D1049878

Sharing Information with Employees

Toward Understanding in Industry

Sharing Information with Employees

By

Alexander R. Heron

STANFORD UNIVERSITY PRESS
STANFORD UNIVERSITY, CALIFORNIA

LONDON: HUMPHREY MILFORD
OXFORD UNIVERSITY PRESS

STANFORD UNIVERSITY PRESS
STANFORD UNIVERSITY, CALIFORNIA

LONDON: HUMPHREY MILFORD
OXFORD UNIVERSITY PRESS

THE BAKER AND TAYLOR COMPANY
55 FIFTH AVENUE, NEW YORK

PRINTED AND BOUND IN THE UNITED STATES
OF AMERICA BY STANFORD UNIVERSITY PRESS

FOREWORD

THIS book represents an enormously important contribution to material in the field of industrial relations and personnel management. We have, for years past, had shelves well filled with books on general or special phases of the employer-employee relation, and additions to our libraries on this subject are continuing to expand with incredible and even alarming rapidity. In spite of all this mass of material there has always been a peculiar gap, which Mr. Heron has now admirably filled. For, strange as it may seem, while all of our general or special works on labor relations, personnel management, and similar subjects have discussed in great detail how to employ specific techniques, none of them have more than touched on the most fundamental of all techniques in the labor management field: how to convey information to employees. None of them have ever thought it necessary to attempt to answer such questions as: How do you tell employees what you are doing or proposing to do? How do you tell them about the business in which they are engaged? How do you tell them the importance of the project on which they are working?

These, and a variety of similar questions, have remained unanswered because it was assumed, apparently, that everyone knew the answers instinctively. And everyone was presumed to know the answers because everyone knew how to read and could understand the spoken word. Consequently, it was assumed that if employees were given something to read or were told something that this was all that was needed to carry over the idea of the writer or speaker. In other words, the information had been conveyed. But, in fact, this was precisely the trouble in all too many instances; for the problem, as Mr. Heron so graphically points out and particularly emphasizes in his title, is not how to convey information but how to share it. Now sharing and conveying are in no sense synonomous, for sharing calls into play social ideas and relations that are entirely absent when something is merely conveyed. Conveying is mechanical; sharing is personal.

Implicit throughout Mr. Heron's treatment is consideration of the business as a social institution as well as an organization designed to carry out economic objectives. And since it is a social institution, many of its practical controls must be determined on the basis of subjective considerations. Viewed from this aspect, and but for one very good reason, this book might well have had as a subtitle "A Manual of Social Psychology for Business Institutions." Such a title, however, would have been pretentious; and you can't share information with employees and be pretentious. This book demonstrates that if any such element is present, the effort will not be a sharing but only a futile dissemination.

Mr. Heron is no theoretical practitioner but is well known to many as Director of Industrial Relations for a large and far-flung enterprise. Here, over a decade or more, he has successfully proved that the methods he suggests are the methods which make the sharing of information as between management and workers not only a regular and an accepted but also—what is of even more importance to both—an acceptable process.

It probably can be said that, above everything else, Mr. Heron has demonstrated in practice, and has now committed his demonstration to writing, that the indispensable ingredients in any successful industrial relations program, whether in the phase of sharing information or in any of its other aspects, are candor and honesty as between the parties. The successful employer-employee relation also has implicit within it acceptance of the principle that there is a mutuality of obligation and responsibility that in the successful enterprise continually flows through well-worn channels in both directions: from the top down and from the bottom up; and that neither direction of movement is of greater importance than the other. The sharing of information is one of the most important management devices to assure that these channels shall be reasonably free of much of the extraneous material that ordinarily tends to clog them. Where this is true—that is, where they are free—the problem of management is incalculably simplified. For a nation at war it is vital that in as many business institutions as possible this should be true. This book should help to make it true in many more places.

PAUL ELIEL

STANFORD UNIVERSITY
January 8, 1942

AUTHOR'S ACKNOWLEDGMENT

Because nothing in this book is new or original, it involves a debt to a large number of people whose experiences, philosophies, and advice it borrows and repeats. That debt is here acknowledged with gratitude but without specifying individuals. Two acknowledgments are demanded by my conscience. The first is to a group of more than a hundred and fifty industrialists who sat with me through an earnest conference at Burlington, Vermont, in 1940. Not only did they contribute much of the material for the book, but they prompted the search for a book on the subject. We found no such book; so their contributions have been combined and supplemented to make this one. The second is to Miss Frieda Parkman for cheerful and valuable assistance in the preparation of the manuscript.

ALEXANDER R. HERON

CONTENTS

INTRODUCTION

The number of persons who have a positive desire to inflict injury on other persons is probably so small as to be negligible. Those persons for whom the discomfort, suffering, or poverty of others is an object in itself are an insignificant fraction of mankind.

But those who inflict injury and suffering on others not as an end but as a means to another end, those who attack in the spirit of defense, those who restrict the prosperity, growth, and liberty of others in their effort to promote their own prosperity, growth, and liberty — they are legion. Their "inhumanities to man," sometimes ruthless, sometimes merely blind, have created in our world a hell of which Lucifer himself must be proud.

The children of one nation have grown to manhood and womanhood in the delusion that their chance for life and comfort depends on their ability to crush the men and women of a neighbor nation. They believe that beyond an imaginary political line called "the border" lives a race of men and women who hate them and seek their destruction. And the fruit of this belief, rooted in the soil of ignorance, fertilized by distorted knowledge, is a crusade to destroy the neighbor nation and so protect their own.

The children of one "race" have been infused with contempt and hatred for another "race," or all other "races," a contempt and hatred distilled from fear of the supposed threat to their own welfare through the existence and welfare of these others. Boys and girls whom they have never known become their enemies; ways of life which they have never seen, identified in symbols and slogans, become the objects of their fanatical intolerance.

Within a single nation or community, casually allied persons have come to think of themselves as a group or class whose interests demand the restriction, suppression, or even the destruction of other persons whom they picture as another group or class. Individuals who are without malice or cruelty have accepted a group intolerance for some other class, which they do not picture as an aggregation of individuals very like themselves. Lacking knowledge of, or even contact with, the individuals involved, they have accepted a collection of inaccurate generalizations and meaningless symbols concerning them.

Men organized into unions as wage earners have adopted for themselves the symbol of "labor" and in an emotional devotion to common self-interest have demonstrated bitter antagonism toward other individuals whom they likewise carelessly group and loosely label. They believe that their own welfare is impeded or threatened by those whose savings provide the places in which they work, the tools which they use, and the channels through which their wages come. Not knowing these people as persons, they group them into an imaginary class, call them "capital," condemn them as an enemy class, and carry on a crusade against them in the sincere belief that the crusade is demanded by their own self-interest.

Persons possessed of property in the form of shares of stock in corporations, though not organized into any kind of union, have come to look upon themselves as the "investor class." In this class character they have developed or accepted a fear of "labor." They have accepted a concept which makes organized labor their enemy, an enemy seeking to deprive them of the fair rental for their savings and even to destroy their property. And so they, too, have mentally enlisted in a crusade, of prayer at least, for the suppression of this enemy class. Their symbols for the enemy include "racketeer" and "goon."

Persons engaged in the management of business or industrial enterprise also are inclined to develop a vague concept of themselves as a class and a definite concept of organized labor as an enemy class. Fearing the invasion of their own "prerogatives" (another symbol) or the resistance to the effectiveness of their management, they are constantly on guard. Usually negative in their resistance, they sometimes carry on aggression as a form of better defense. They oppose the progress of wage earners who in the aggregate are the customers for their products and services.

Between nations we have seen battles on land, on sea, and in the air. We have seen the sinking of merchant ships, the bombing of civilian populations, the blockade of enemy countries in the effort to force starvation on men, women, and children. Within a nation we have seen strikes, sabotage, and boycotts, the stoning of factory windows by the men who yesterday worked by the light through those windows. We have seen lockouts, discharges, injunctions, blacklists. We have seen mass picketing and mass arrests. We have seen appeals to mass emotion on behalf of the "right to work," and counter appeals on behalf of the "right to decent working conditions."

These hate-crusades, class symbols, and fear complexes are not exactly the same as the war psychology of other centuries. They differ in their intensity and in their voluntary enlistments as the Crusades of the Middle Ages differed from the conquests of Julius Caesar.

The fear complex against another nation, race, or class is born of suspicion of the motives of the people who are the group behind the enemy symbol. This suspicion is the product of lack of knowledge of the human beings who are that group. This lack of knowledge is the natural result of lack of contact in the complexity of modern political and industrial affairs, a lack due in part at least to the sizes of the units involved.

A House of Representatives with 435 members is not a group in which personal understanding will flourish, all the more since the average member of Congress represents a district of a third of a million population. There can likewise be little understanding between the 200,000 employees and the 400,000 stockholders of our largest corporation. The old units of contact, social, political and industrial, have been so expanded or obscured that they no longer function. The family home is obscured by the city house or apartment. The town meeting has been superseded by the million-dollar campaign. The farmer market has been superseded by the mammoth packing-house company or the mammoth marketing co-operative. The small industrial or business enterprise has largely given place to the giant corporation.

This book humbly suggests one channel for rebuilding understanding between man and man, in American industry, without which the American way of life cannot survive no matter what victories may be won in battle. Wars and political campaigns have not removed the basic fault of lack of understanding with its resultant suspicion, intolerance, and hatred. Strikes, lockouts, and legal procedures have done nothing to restore understanding and goodwill in industry, within the nation which is perhaps freest from the virus of fear.

Unless understanding can be achieved between the individuals and so-called "classes" within American industry and business, our boasted way of life is in danger. This danger is within, and is as real and immediate as any threat from the ideologies beyond the seas. We may see the symbol of democracy win another war against the symbol of dictatorship. But unless we can restore among ourselves the understanding of our common interest in our daily economic life, the victory will belong to the symbol of democracy, not to the reality of democracy.

The effort and cost and suffering of the struggle now thrust upon us will demand—and receive—the absolute maximum of personal dedication and nation-wide co-operation. Suspicion and antagonism between groups is relegated to the area of inconsequential details. Even to the most conservative mind, there is little reason for management to demur at sharing information with employees. The range of information which is necessarily confidential for military reasons is obvious. The usually guarded facts involving costs, profits, taxes, and similar matters are clearly not worth guarding today. There has surely never been a time when the actual facts were so definitely of such a nature that we want everyone to know them.

Minds of employees are keenly alert to facts. There is full employment at high wages. Millions who have been almost unconscious of taxes are becoming aware of the personal burden. Every man, woman, and youth who is part of America is passionately anxious to see the American productive system function as never before.

Some day there will be the aftermath. There will be curtailment of defense activity, demobilization, unemployment, confusion, a puzzled sense of let-down. There will be a need of national and international grand strategy to plan for the rebuilding of a war-torn world. For such plans to mature there must be a firm and understanding faith in all the land. There must be mutual understanding, and the mutual confidence which is its companion.

While we have no ax to grind, no facts worth concealing, no group antagonisms to overcome, employers can build a habit and a method of sharing information with employees which will insure the mutual understanding and confidence needed for the next phase of the "epic of America."

We may be living through a basic change in our method of life, a social evolution so "speeded up" as to be in fact a revolution. We may have no conception of the economy within which we shall live, work, produce, and consume just a few years hence. We may not know the extent to which we shall be regimented for the needs of war, nor the extent to which that regimentation may be relaxed or reversed when the crisis has passed. We may not safely speculate on the future ownership or control of this natural resource, that means of production, or some other instrument of distribution. We can merely speculate as to the survival of production for profit as against production for use.

But this we do know: Regardless of the form of economy or of government, there will be work to do. The functions of production and distribution will go on. Tasks will be subdivided, and there will be those who direct and manage and those who accept direction and perform the work. Between these managers and workers, understanding will always be the needed link. Without this understanding, no ideology will survive, no social structure will serve, no economic system will produce our homes and clothes and food.

I

THE EMPLOYEE'S INTEREST IN THE ENTERPRISE

Employers are often heard bemoaning the fact that employees do not take an interest in their work; that their only concerns seem to be higher wages, shorter hours, better working conditions. The facts support the complaint. But we do not generally agree on the causes back of the facts.

Many employers, many "successful" men of the old school, see the cause in the general softening of our way of life: Men have lost their sense of self-reliance. Through organization and through governmental paternalism or employer paternalism they have come to depend on outside forces rather than their own efforts.

Others believe the mind of the average worker has been poisoned by the propaganda of agitators and demagogues. They believe he has accepted the disruptive doctrine of the class struggle and has come to believe that his interests are opposed to those of his employer. They point to numerous cases where workers have seriously damaged the enterprise in which they work, in the supposed effort to improve their own welfare.

Some observers look upon the worker's lack of interest in his work as a natural result of the increased size of the employing unit and the accompanying specialization of work. The increased size has made it difficult for the individual to comprehend the enterprise as a whole. The subdivision of operating processes and the specialization of work have made it difficult for him to comprehend the process as a whole and his part in it. Both difficulties tend to reduce his interest in his own work, either as a factor of economic importance or as an outlet for man's creative instinct.

Still other observers believe that the large modern industrial enterprise has systematically withheld from the wage earner all information which would stimulate his interest in his work as part of the larger pattern. This denial, according to this view, has left the worker nothing to be interested in except his wages, hours, and comfort.

Whatever the cause, people recognize a lack of interest on the part of most workers in the productive features of their work. Whatever the cure, most thoughtful employers and observers feel the dominant need of getting the worker interested in his work in a broad sense. They feel that he must be enabled to recognize that, beyond a fair share in the money results of the enterprise, he has a "stake" in the success of the enterprise itself.

And, whatever the cause, we here offer the prescription for at least a first part of the cure: Sharing information with employees will permit them to understand in some measure that they cannot prosper without the prosperity of the business or institution with which they have affiliated themselves.

In the social-economic code of Moses, there is an injunction to lenders of money: "No man shall take the nether or the upper millstone to pledge: for he taketh a man's life to pledge." The same principle found expression in the common law of England and in the statutory law of most of the United States. Certain personal possessions, usually essential to livelihood or to the practice of a trade or profession, were made exempt from execution. An artisan's tools, a blacksmith's anvil, or a physician's horse and buggy must not be seized for debt.

Failure to translate the ancient principle into the language and conditions of modern life is illustrated by one significant fact: Almost a generation after the doctor's horse and buggy had ceased to exist, the doctor's horse and buggy were still exempt from execution but statutory law had not yet made the doctor's automobile exempt.

To the manual worker, the march of time has brought an even greater change, with even less translation of ancient principles into modern language. The upper and the nether millstones now are owned by the Mammoth Flouring Mills or Gigantic Foods Corporation. The artisan's tools and the blacksmith's anvil are owned by Colossal Motors Limited or by Worldwide Steel Corporation. Instead of his grist mill, the miller's son owns a number on a payroll. Instead of his hammer and anvil, the blacksmith's son possesses a brass check with a number on it.

What is needed to induce the miller's son and the blacksmith's son to regard these numbers, these jobs of theirs, with the same care and interest their fathers gave to the grist mill and to the hammer and anvil and forge? What will help the worker of today to see his job as something akin to the tools and workbench his father owned? How can he grasp the fact that as his father cared for his tools, solicitously, almost affectionately, so he must care for, and protect, the job which is the modern form of the artisan's livelihood? Can he perceive that as his father the cabinet maker and his father's father before him guarded the reputation of their shop for the honest quality of the chairs they made, so he must in his own interest guard the reputation of the larger "shop" of which he is a part, the larger shop of which a part—a job—belongs to him?

For that matter, how many of us, as employers, have recognized that a place on our payroll, a job in our plant, is the only "property" the average worker possesses from which to derive his livelihood? We deplore the fact that he does not seem to take an interest in his job; we overlook the fact that we have seldom shown him that we recognize that he *has* an interest in his job—a possessive interest, if you please. Until he can recognize this possessive interest, he is not likely to take an interest in the job in the sense of putting himself into it, protecting and fostering it in all its relationships.

If we had fully recognized the interest in the job which belongs to the worker, perhaps we should have done much more to tell him about the features of the job which do not come to his attention in his highly specialized function—perhaps the function of watching four automatic machines turning out twenty units per minute of the precision-tooled cam which eventually goes into position 23A.

Perhaps we should have given him a chance to see, or at least read about, the structure of the finished product and the place and importance of his specialized piece or part. Perhaps we should have let him know the important characteristics of the steel he handles and where it is made. Perhaps we should have told him the market outlook and how much "livelihood" his job promises for next year. Perhaps we should hope to have him know the burden of taxes borne by his job, what the highly paid executive does to insure the existence of each job in the enterprise, and a hundred other facts.

The employee in our picture *has* a right, title, and interest in his job, but only if he has earned it. He has a claim on the enterprise which makes his job exist, but only if he has paid for that claim. We must acknowledge his claim and his interest, as our payment for the interest we are asking him to put into his job. But we are not advancing this acknowledgment before he has made his investment. He has made it just as really as his father paid in money for the tools and equipment of his little shop and paid in skill and honesty for its reputation and good will.

If a casual worker agrees with us to work for eight hours, at sixty cents an hour, cleaning out the storeroom, we can close the account with him at the end of eight hours. He has given us eight hours of honest work as he agreed. We have given him $4.80 as we agreed. He owes us no more; we owe him no more. But if he comes to work on a regular job, a so-called permanent job starting at sixty cents an hour, a different story unfolds. At the first payday the stories look alike.

In the week he has given us forty hours of honest work, as he agreed. We have given him $24.00 as we agreed. Perhaps he owes us nothing more and we owe him nothing more that can be recognized at that time. But even then there is a subtle difference: The day before he was hired he had no conceivable claim on us different from that of any other applicant being considered for the job. When he was hired, he received from us an opportunity to qualify for a continuing job. We received from him the implied commitment to try to fit into our way of work, to learn our methods, and to remain with us and give us the benefit of his continued learning. But it takes months and years to show the real difference between this story and the story of the man who came to work for just one day.

Assume that the second man was twenty-five years old the day he came to work. He "fitted in," he learned our ways, he gained experience, he acquired new skills, he took on new responsibilities. As he did so, his rate of pay was fairly increased. As the years pass he is suddenly forty years old—above the average age of employees in American industry. He has been our employee for fifteen years. His present rate of pay is $1.00 an hour. His average rate for the fifteen years has been eighty cents. He has given us 30,000 hours of honest work. We have paid him $24,000, at the successively agreed rates. Can we close the books with him? Can we say he has given us the agreed hours, we have paid the agreed dollars, and there is no more owing, by him or by us?

He has put into the job more than the 30,000 hours. He has put into it, into the enterprise, fifteen years of his life. They are not just fifteen years, either; they are *the* fifteen years which should be the foundation of all of his later life earnings. Those years are his investment in the enterprise. We cannot give them back to him. We can pay off a bondholder, or buy out a stockholder; but we cannot buy out the investment this worker has made. We wanted him to stay with us and put in those years. We want him now, as through those years, to protect and promote the business which is his job, as if it were his own. And it is his own in a way which neither he nor we can change. He is not the same man at forty that he was at twenty-five; the difference has been invested in this enterprise.

True, he has gained in some ways. He has gained skills, knowledge, maturity. He may have gained some reputation for special expertness in some line. He may have money in the bank, an equity in his home or in a life insurance policy. On the other hand, he has lost youth, adaptability, salability. He has lost fifteen years of the promise of future usefulness to any enterprise. He has risked or staked his chances of employment and income, during middle age and later years, on the future soundness and success of this enterprise. He can take away with him his acquired skills, knowledge, and reputation; he cannot withdraw the investment of the years of his youth. The important question is, has he invested those years or merely spent them?

The case is tragic when a man so invests his priceless years in an enterprise which goes merrily on without him, exploiting the youth of newer, younger men. The case is tragic; but it is very rare. I can honestly say that I have never known of any man "fired-at-forty" who was not fired for reasons unrelated to his age. On the contrary, I have known scores and hundreds of men who should have been fired, who would have been fired if they had been thirty years old, but who were retained because they were forty or over when the potential causes for discharge became known.

We employers assume that the employee of long standing has been fairly treated as to retention of his job, as in all other ways. We have been able to free him from the fear of losing his job, his membership in the enterprise, to some other man. Now, with him, we must plan and work to eliminate his fear of losing his job through the death of that portion of the enterprise which represents his job. We have found a way to assure him that as long as that part of the business which is his job continues to exist, his equity in it will continue to be recognized. Now we must not only permit but invite him to work with us to see that the business and his particular job-section of it continue to exist.

We must face facts together and see that failure to improve the efficiency of the enterprise is a sure way to destroy it—not only his job-section of it, but all the rest of the business. If we so manage the enterprise that his job "folds up" when he is forty or forty-two or forty-seven, we have permitted him to put his best years into a business which he subconsciously considered safe only to find his investment wiped out —to find that his years have been spent, not invested.

The major tragedy occurs where not one man but many deposit priceless years in an enterprise which they all discover, too late, is unsound. In a year when their habits have become fixed and their heads partly gray, their ages are from forty to fifty, and their periods of employment have reached ten, twenty, or thirty years, they find that the enterprise is not the lifetime security they thought they were buying.

This places on us an obligation, the mutual understanding of which is the key to constructive co-operation. That is the obligation so to plan and manage the enterprise that it will be the anchorage for middle age which the worker has a right to expect.

When we undertake our duty to investors of money, we see clearly the obligation to preserve for them a continuing enterprise, one which in twenty years will have a physical plant not only well maintained but modernized, a product kept abreast of customer demand by means of research, an adequate supply of raw materials, processes in line with technical progress, the continued confidence of customers, and a personnel in management, production, and sales which has reproduced itself, has trained its understudies.

We have not always recognized that this forward-looking management is part of our debt to employees as truly as to stockholders, that we must render this service to the investor of years as much as to the investor of dollars.

It is small wonder that the employee has not always recognized that which we have not always recognized ourselves. If he knows that research and depreciation and public goodwill, modernization and intelligent personnel practices, adequate reserves and the "plowing back" of part of the earnings are the elements which insure the existence of the enterprise and *his* job in the years to come, he is going to take an interest in that job and that enterprise in the way we want him to—and invest himself in it.

It is relatively easy to supervise and induce employees to do a fair amount of competent work day by day. It is difficult to induce them to put themselves, wisely and wholeheartedly, into the lasting success of the enterprise. Money alone will not do it. These things are indispensable:

First, we must recognize our inescapable obligation to manage the enterprise in such a way as to furnish middle-age security for those who spend their years of youth in the enterprise as wage earners.

Second, we must encourage them to expect and demand this kind of management as their truest form of social security.

Third, we must share with them the information which will create this attitude and which will continuously show them whether or not their long-time interests are being conserved.

Then and only then can we expect to find them shaping their attitudes and actions in terms of the future security of the enterprise in which they have such a priceless stake.

II

THE BASIS OF UNDERSTANDING

We Americans are not sentimental people. We pride ourselves on being practical and realistic: We have accepted the scientific method in most phases of our modern life; we have recorded observations, tangible facts, hypotheses, experiments; we have hardly winced under the accusation that we have moved from practicalism to pragmatism and that we have become worshipers of measurable results. There are items of evidence to the contrary. But in spite of our occasional lapses into sentiment or emotion, we probably must classify ourselves as realists, in so far as we can appraise our mass characteristics.

The large majority of us who are wage earners have no choice. If we render service for pay, if we are "gainfully employed" in the language of the census, we are compelled to be realists. The pay or the "gain" may come to us as a check or as money in an envelope; we have no time to worry about the theory of money. The reality which we have "gained" for our work is a place in which to live by renting it or by making payments on its mortgage. It is food for the family, clothing for us and the children, gasoline for the car. Those of us whose incomes fix—and fix narrowly—the standard of our living must be realists. We have emphasized this fact by calling our wages or salaries not our "income" but our "living."

From this almost unanimous attitude among wage earners, springs a concept that any "income" which is not earned as wages is not a "living." Without going to the extent of denying the right of capital to a profit, the practical wage earner cannot conceive of the bondholder's interest or the stockholder's dividends as a "living." The day-to-day life of the typical wage earner does not promise an old age when he can hope to possess a fund saved out of the present scant "living." His imagination cannot run to a day when his own "living" will be the interest on the savings from his earlier earnings, to the day when his abilities to "earn a living" have been used up.

Millions of typical wage earners have accepted the fact and the promise of the Federal Social Security Law without relating it to the kind of savings which create capital. In the amended program it is difficult to demonstrate any such relationship; old-age pensions paid practically from current taxes do not illustrate the accumulation and employment of a capital fund and the utilization of its earnings. But in the early days of the law, when the reserve fund principle was its foundation, too many employers destroyed the greatest object lesson of the age in the fundamentals of capital. They denied the existence of any reserve fund, because the money, invested in securities of the United States, was being used for current expenses. They neglected to explain that the same is true of money similarly invested by banks and insurance companies. They neglected to concentrate their wrath on the spending itself, regardless of how the money was acquired or borrowed. Above all, they neglected the opportunity to demonstrate that the employee covered by social security was, by compulsion, a capitalist; that he, in co-operation with all others similarly covered, was actually accumulating a capital fund; and that this capital fund was essentially the same in nature as that which had been invested in the plant and equipment which created his own job. Employers thus participated in the subsequent change which enables the worker to believe more than ever in the magic of taxes and the benevolence of government.

Thus, the realistic employee sees earnings only as the result of current labor and as the provision for current living needs. Capital is his enemy. The bondholder or stockholder is a capitalist. Vaguely, a capitalist is a parasite. A larger

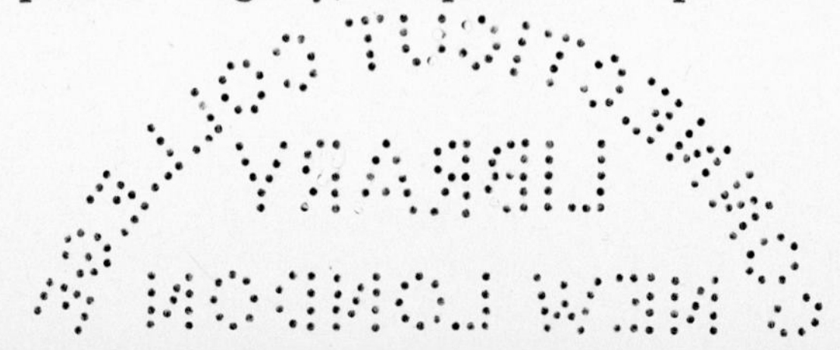

share, perhaps all, of the production of industry should go currently to the workers who produce. Labor is the only source of wealth and production.

Of course, if he understood the laws of economics, he might identify capital as the product of labor not currently consumed but saved to supply the tools for greater production. But he probably has had no opportunity for study of the abstract science of economics, and, being now by necessity a hardened realist, he is deaf to all theories of abstract economics.

From our employer point of view, this wage-earner attitude is one of tragic misunderstanding. And so it is. It is the foundation of every conflict which retards, interrupts, and damages our industrial and business enterprise. It is the substance of the only hope which has ever encouraged the preachers of subversive doctrines in America.

Because the wage earner is and must be a realist, we cannot achieve a relationship of understanding by talking to him in the language of economics. To him that language is not the language of his realism. The language he must use in his real life deals with the price of groceries, the date the rent is due, the amount of the doctor's bill, the wearing-out of clothes.

Are we, as employers, willing to be typically American and realistic? Are we ready to see that our free-enterprise system is doomed unless it can be understood by the great majority of its citizens, constituents, and beneficiaries? Are we realistic enough to admit the compulsion of securing real understanding between wage earners and those who manage the tools of production supplied by the savings of past production?

Understanding is the fruit of knowledge, the result of reasoning from known facts. The knowledge which is real to the wage earner is knowledge of tangible things, not book knowledge or theories.

The place and responsibility of management in the present situation becomes clearer if we realize that the wage earner once had the knowledge which brings understanding and that the growth of our industrial system has deprived him of that knowledge, the very growth which gives us pride and confidence in the principles of free enterprise. In the age when the worker had this understanding, it was the product of his intimate knowledge of real things and of his consciousness of the relation of that knowledge to himself as an individual.

The foundation for any program for understanding between us and our employees is a complete respect on our part for the personality and individuality of the employee. While there may be a hundred or a hundred thousand employees on our payroll, and while we may bargain collectively with them through their chosen representatives, our relations are not with a mass of men; our relations are with each one of a hundred or a hundred thousand individual persons. We cannot share information with an abstract, imaginary entity such as "the public," "labor," or "the union," or "the rank and file." We can share information with Al Adams and Bill Brown and Carl Casey and Dan Davis, who work with us and receive their incomes in wages which we deliver to them.

We need not go far back in our American industrial history to find the productive unit of organization in which knowledge and understanding were complete, and the personality of the worker significant. Let us turn our imaginations for a few minutes toward the place and time of that understanding in industry. Let us picture it so clearly that the image will remain with us throughout our troubled study of the misunderstanding in industry today.

It was a time and place in which the realism of the worker's mind was in contact with the realities of the industrial enterprise, in which his innocence of abstract economics did not involve a baffled attitude of misunderstanding. It was a time and place in which his instinctive individuality was not in conflict with the mass psychology of mass employment and mass production.

We might find our picture of the old understanding in a wagon shop, a grist mill, a cotton mill, a pottery or cutlery shop. Let us find it in a furniture shop. Perhaps eight men work there. One of them is the boss. He owns the shop, but he works there, visibly. The other seven receive wages. The work done by the boss is not all done with tools; sometimes he uses a pencil. He draws designs, writes occasional letters, puts down figures about wages, costs, and prices.

The other seven know, quite closely, how much money the boss had saved up from his earnings as a journeyman before he started in business for himself; in other words, how much "capital" he had and how long it took him to save it up.

The shop or factory is on the same lot as the house where the boss lives; he owns it. The other seven know how much his taxes are each year. They helped to build the ten-by-thirty addition to the shop last year, and they know how much that cost. They were all in on the discussion before the new lathe was bought, and they remember the price and the freight. They remember how the boss borrowed some of the money from his wife's sister.

They know that the dining-room "suit" on which they are working now is for Jane Winton, that used to be Jane Carey, the schoolteacher, before she married Bill Winton, the banker. They know it has to be as good as the furniture she saw in Buffalo, and that if it is good Bill's mother is going to give the boss an order for another lot which will keep them all busy through the winter.

They see the finished job emerging under their skilled hands, day by day. They know how difficult it was to get the seasoned walnut, and what it finally cost, what price is to be paid for the finished job, how much the boss will "make" on it, and how much of that will go to pay off the loan from the sister-in-law.

They know that the boss has gradually built a reputation for honest quality and skilled workmanship and that they are part of that reputation. They know why once in a while they have had to wait for a little for their wages—when the taxes had to be paid before the money came in for the new counter and fixtures at the drugstore.

Above all, they know the boss. Their attachment to him is basically not sentimental but practical. He is the salesman who gets the orders which bring work to them. He collects the money which pays their wages. He manages to accumulate the working space and the equipment. They are realistic enough to know that they can get their full and fair share of the income of the business. They laugh at anyone who talks of the conflict between labor and capital, between them and the boss.

They know. Because they know, they understand. And in that full and simple understanding they "put themselves" into every job.

It is a picture which calls forth, from most of us, a sigh for the good old days—a picture which, in general, has gone forever. And yet the essential elements of it must be restored to American industry if the free-enterprise system, or even the American level of living, is to survive. And they must be restored before some very early tomorrow!

Some elements of that picture will not and need not return. We cannot maintain our level of living on the hand products or the simple machine products of eight-man factories. Corporate ownership need not give way to the old individual ownership. Indeed establishments of the size we need today can be created only out of the investments of hundreds or thousands of corporate stockholders. The responsibility of the management group to those investors is an added guaranty to wage earners—a guaranty of continuity based on good management, good planning for future supplies, sales, and good will.

No, the essential elements which must be recaptured are not those of the size of the enterprise or the form of ownership. They are the elements of personal significance and knowledge and understanding. As we consider the wisdom and necessity of rebuilding this understanding, the constant reminder of that old picture will keep us thinking clearly. Over and over it will reappear in our discussion of sharing information with employees. In one light it shows the perfect sharing of information—natural, frank, willing. In another light it shows the perfect channel of sharing information—the personal contact group, a few men and their leader. True, this group in modern industry will not be the whole establishment. But within every establishment, such a group relationship, multiplied or repeated many times, will be the channel of the needed knowledge, the area of the needed understanding.

III

WHY NOT TELL THEM?

There are honest objections to sharing information with employees. These, and the reasoning behind them, must not be lightly disregarded. Some of the objections relate to information on certain subjects or types of subjects. Some of these will be mentioned in our discussion of what information may be shared with employees. We are here concerned with objections to the general idea of sharing information with employees.

In spite of the fact that most executives in American enterprise have risen from the ranks, many of them secretly believe that there is a difference between their own mentalities and those of the men of today who are in the ranks. They feel vaguely, and sometimes say definitely, that the rank and file cannot understand the information which management can give them.

This belief can neither be ignored nor denied. It may be sound as to a great portion of the men and women who work for wages. But most of the executives with the superior minds will not argue that things *should* be so. They will not assert that this general inability to understand is a good foundation for the structure of our democracy or a healthy condition among people who are trying to govern themselves. They will say it is too bad, but it just happens to be true; that we may not like it but cannot alter it; that some people are just born that way.

Granting the truth of this position as far as we must, there are some answers which should be made.

Are some people just born without the ability to understand? Some people? All of us were born that way. We were also born without the ability to walk; but we learned by trying. We were born without the ability to talk, or read, or write; but we learned, by trying as we were given the chance. So did the employees who now work for us. Incidentally, they were born without the ability to do the work for which we now hire them; but they learned that as they were given the opportunity.

How much opportunity have managers given wage earners to understand the enterprises in which they are both engaged? Managers have no God-given superiority in this respect. They have had to learn to understand this same information. They have learned; but they learned gradually. Few of them when they first put on white collars and sat down at desks, could have reasoned to any correct conclusions if they had been handed all the information they now use every day.

We have no right to say that our fellow workers cannot understand until they have had a chance to learn, until they have had the information to consider. Moreover, they should have access not to a confusing flood of facts, but to facts as their interest prompts them to reach for the information. Admitting that inability to understand business information is characteristic of employees, is not the experiment of sharing some information with them worth trying? Is it not worth hoping that with practice and opportunity they will learn to understand, as they have learned to walk, talk, read, write, and work?

But in addition to those who believe it true but regrettable that employees cannot understand such information as we are discussing, there are others who believe it true but not regrettable. They also will say that some people are just born that way, and they will go on to imply that this is in accordance with some divine plan. It seems to them inevitable that human society be classified or stratified, in the same manner as a hive of bees: If all bees were workers, there would be no organization under qualified leadership. If all were queens, there would be no honey. If all human beings were endowed by nature with keen, alert, understanding minds, none of us would be satisfied to work for wages or at manual tasks; we would all want to be bosses.

This attitude has a lot of history behind it. It is the idea of both ancient and modern tyrannies under which conquered enemies became the slaves of the conquerors. It is the idea of the medieval aristocracies with their ruling classes. Many of those who express this view consider themselves devoted to the American doctrine of freedom of opportunity. They can even rationalize their implied belief in a predestined working class with their devotion to the democratic ideal. They can maintain that the status of any member of that working class was not forced upon him by some other group in society, but is rather the result of his natural endowments. For such a man, equality of opportunity is the opportunity to use his own individual capacities, rather than opportunity to achieve in a field for which he is not fitted. Therefore, our imaginary aristocrat will rationalize that such a man can have equality of opportunity only when others differently endowed by nature, plan for him, lead and direct his work, and allot to him his fair reward.

Every social order in history which has been built on the foundation of such an idea has collapsed because its foundation refused to remain stable very long. The supposedly predestined working class has successively won the right to bear arms, to own land, to choose among religions, to read and write, to choose its work, and, finally, to rule its nation by its votes. We have long since learned that proper exercise of the right to rule by vote involves abundant opportunity to know the facts and conditions with which the ruling and the votes must deal. The deliberate effort to share business information with the great majority who work for wages corresponds closely to the deliberate plan to make education, basic and continued education, freely available to all people.

There is a related but different objection to sharing information with employees, namely, that they do not need it. This objection implies that even if workers can understand it or can learn to understand it, and even if they are not predestined to remain under the guidance of others, the fact still remains that they do not need the information which management does need. Workers are not called upon to make decisions about the conduct of the business, about location, purchasing, sales policies, expansion, new products, research, or advertising. If they will do their share of the work, under the instructions of those whose job is instruction, they will get their wages. They will be happier and better workers if they do not bother about the facts on which these decisions are based. They will even be happier than those who must have these facts and make these decisions. The decisions are both a duty and prerogative of management which management cannot evade. Therefore, the required facts are to be left in the hands of management, not in the hands of those who cannot use them.

Perhaps in this reasoning we are trying to set the conditions on which we expect employees to sell us their time, strength, skill, and service. And maybe we may not get what we expect, in return for wages alone. For the argument, while quite sound perhaps in some respects, is faulty in several important particulars. First, it is inconceivable that any of us will do his work as well without some understanding of its purpose, its place in the work of the world. Second, the lack of this information has reached a point where it has resulted in misunderstandings and conflicts within our industrial order which not only restrict the effectiveness but threaten the very existence of the order. Third, and closely related, we have all of us, every adult citizen, been jointly and equally entrusted with the government of our nation, state, and city. That government is increasingly engaged in the protection and regulation of the economic interests of all of us. It is inconceivable that the forty millions of us who work for wages can do a good job, or even a safe job, of governing by votes, without knowing more and more about our economic interests.

The belief that millions of our fellow workers will be better and happier workers if they do as they are told, without the understanding of the enterprise as something larger than their jobs, is a disease which has already weakened our economic and political society. It is a belief which has been encouraged and to some extent validated by our mass-production methods. The creation of hundreds of identical jobs has seemed to call for the employment of hundreds of identical men. To be identical in relation to the job, it is maintained, their knowledge should be equally limited to that necessary for the performance of the job; the acquisition of broader knowledge would result in harmful variations among them, in their thinking, in their ambitions, in their attitudes toward the work.

The reasoning traced above contains its own refutation. The hundreds of men similarly employed think differently when given the same facts; therefore they are not identical men but are individuals, equipped with individual minds. Time after time in history the regimentation of men has been disrupted because men are individuals. For years, perhaps for generations, regimentation can succeed; it always ends in one of two ways.

The first results from wide acceptance of the idea that the persons are not individuals but are members of a class, that their personalities are not important but their class adherence is important. That result achieved, some leader makes an appeal to the class consciousness which the ruling class has created and inspires a physical revolt in the interest of the class or the "proletariat." Or a demagogue arises to exploit the class consciousness in a political class revolt.

The second way involves providing open doors whereby the otherwise regimented persons may move freely in accordance with their individual capacities and ambitions. The obvious chance for any individual to escape the dead level of the class in which he stands today prevents that class from becoming fixed as such. The class which experiences individual progress and graduation is never one to which the demagogue, the revolutionist, or the dictator can long appeal.

A currently well-known radical, who describes himself as a "militant labor leader," made an assertion some two years ago which unwittingly revealed how vulnerable his demagoguery is to this attack through the open door. Three or four members of his "rank and file" union had been promoted to supervisory salaried positions. He made the charge before a neutral arbitrator that this amounted to employing them as labor spies, that the employers had induced these men to abandon and to agree to betray their brothers of the working class. He conveyed the belief that the wage earners for whom he claimed to speak formed a fixed class and implied that the open door through which an individual might progress constituted a menace to the solidarity and welfare of the class.

The American nation may not be truly a classless society, but it is a society without class barriers. The subversive activities of recent years have exploited chiefly the idea that classes have developed in American society and that boundaries are being firmly fixed between these classes. The ideas of the class struggle could gain no hearing among us until employers had, consciously or otherwise, provided a basis for ideas of classes and class barriers. And the principal way in which employers have fostered this idea has been by permitting the men and women who work for wages to become increasingly ignorant of the wider significance and importance of the work they are doing.

The vast majority of managers and employers have permitted this lack of knowledge on the part of employees without even being conscious of it. Repeatedly we hear them bemoaning the fact that workers do not understand their responsibilities to society, do not understand their interest in the free-enterprise system, do not understand the difference between constructive policies and demagoguery on election day. Perhaps they do not understand chiefly because employers have neglected to share with them the information from which such understanding could arise.

But in these paragraphs our discussion relates to those who have not merely neglected the sharing of information with employees as most of us have neglected it, but to those who, for the reasons outlined above, have decided that sharing information with employees is useless, unnecessary, or undesirable. We have suggested that the spokesmen of that type of reasoning have played into the hands of those subversive agents who seek the destruction of the American system. That is only half the truth. These spokesmen are in themselves a subversive influence. If their reasonings bore full fruit, without the reaction of physical or political revolt, the American idea would be completely extinguished.

The American idea has no place for a class predestined to be wage earners incapable of understanding the world beyond the workbench, no place for a class which is denied the opportunity to reason its conclusions on facts which it helps to create, no place for a class which is happier because ignorant of anything beyond the daily task. And those whose sense of superiority leads them to believe in either the necessity or the desirability of such classes are themselves enemies of the American idea or ignorant of its genius.

For the genius of the American idea is the individuality and importance of the human being, not the crystallization of classes even for class betterment. The very industries which have created the mass employment of regimented workers are the fruits of ideas conceived in the minds of individuals—and usually individual workers. If there is to be like progress in the future of our nation's industries, it will be because men continue to work, to think, and to progress, as individuals.

Therefore, why not tell to the men who work with us the facts which will enable them to contribute to our common progress?

We as employers have facts which will enable them to look beyond the machine to the finished product, its market, its uses, to look behind the machine to the mines and forests and far places from which its raw materials must come. We have facts which will help them to look past the pay check to the broader areas of purchasing power, competitive costs, and stability of employment into old age. We have facts which will help them to see the reality of values in plant capital and research, the benefits of far planning and wise management.

Why not tell them?

IV

THE AGGRESSIVE WILLINGNESS TO SHARE

If we are to explore the what and how of sharing information with employees, we must start with the why. We must understand our own attitude toward such a program. Our reasons will influence the subject matter and our manner of supplying information. Those reasons, and a clear recognition of them by us, will influence the results of our efforts to share information with employees.

There is an attitude best described as one of "reluctant" willingness. Facts once classed as confidential business data are now broadcast through scores of channels. Information once considered sacred is now collected by governmental agencies, analyzed by research agencies, interpreted by professional labor organizers. Inside facts which twenty years ago some corporate managements did not reveal even to their own directors are now available to the average newspaper reader.

It is merely honest to admit that these forced exposures of information once concealed have been the cause of some of our new techniques of reporting to the public, the stockholders, or the employees. The typical financial report to stockholders in 1940 is very different, far franker and more detailed, than that of 1920. More significant, scores of corporations, including many of the largest, now give this same generous information to their employees.

This attitude of the average corporation officer, and its demonstration in the form and distribution of reports, can be fairly expressed thus:

Our stockholders can read the papers and learn how much stock I own or control, and how much salary I draw. Research bureaus can examine certain reports filed with government agencies and sell their analyses and findings. Lawyers may use these in promoting the desires of discontented minority stockholders.

Our employees can read the same news in the papers. But reporters are likely to write it sensationally rather than analytically, and organizers or politicians may present it to our employees in such a way as to create misunderstanding and provoke discontent.

All things considered, we should offset these possibilities by giving the information ourselves to both stockholders and employees.

This is good reasoning, all of it, quite realistic, and sure to lead to an attitude of willingness to share information with employees. But the attitude thus arrived at is negative. It is merely seeking the avoidance of certain undesirable possibilities.

There is also an attitude of "paternalistic" willingness, actually a variation of the benevolent paternalism of the past. The passing type of paternalistic employer did things *for* his employees. He provided free insurance of various kinds, free medical care for employees and their families, free clubhouses and recreational facilities. He sponsored savings and thrift clubs, usually "matching" the interest earnings and sometimes even the deposits. He provided visiting nurses and cooking teachers, plans and plants for employees' gardens. He gave free turkeys at Christmas.

He may have rationalized frankly to the conclusion that this paternalism would buy the abstract thing called "loyalty." More realistically, he may have reasoned that employees who had so much done *for* them would be steady, reliable, grateful, submissive. They would not lightly drift off to other jobs or endanger their status by demanding more wages, joining unions, or otherwise making trouble. Or he may have reasoned that Providence had blessed him with greater fortune, more wealth, more power, more brains. He may have felt a responsibility to provide for "his boys" the things which they were not wise enough to buy—insurance, medical care, and so forth.

Usually, no matter how the paternalist rationalized his attitude of superiority, he refrained from sharing much information with employees. By the first course of reasoning, a little knowledge would be a dangerous thing, they might become discontented in spite of all his generosity. By the second course of reasoning, there was no need to give them much information, since he, the paternalist, had accepted the task of doing most of their thinking for them.

But both courses of reasoning have resulted in willingness to share information with employees. The realistic and selfish paternalist is willing to pass on highly selected information which supports his main effort at keeping employees contented and submissive. And the moral paternalist accepts the task of informing and educating his employees as part of the burden placed on him by Providence. But even in his highly moral attitude there is the danger that he may take himself too seriously; he is likely to feel that his moral obligation includes the task of carefully selecting for his employees the information which he knows they should have and giving them no other.

A third willingness to share information with employees may be described as "propagandist." From this description we exclude all thought of falsehood, so readily associated in our minds with our concept of propaganda. We need not devote even a paragraph to the stupidity or immorality of the employer who conveys false information to his employees, in the effort to create in them an attitude which the truth will not support. When we find an employer capable of such behavior, we find one who is capable of like deception toward his customers, his creditors, and his partners. But the propagandist attitude which we do need to consider aims at the planting of ideas immediately desired by the employer. With no distortion or falsehood in its technique, it relies on selection and interpretation. Those facts which tend to create favorable reactions are selected to be given to the employees. Besides the planting of ideas, an effort is made to cultivate them, often by slightly strained interpretation.

In the sense in which favorable facts are selected for this propaganda program, it follows that unfavorable facts are suppressed. Because it aims at a specific and desired employee reaction, such a program must be like the modern government "information service," a combination of the functions of publicity and censorship. The information given is truthful; the information not given is suppressed because it would not support opinions which the propagandist seeks to present.

The "reluctant" willingness to share information with employees has a slight flavor of castor oil.

The "paternalistic" willingness has some suggestion of the *noblesse oblige* of the old feudal aristocracy.

The "propagandist" willingness has some elements of high-pressure salesmanship.

Each of these forms of willingness to share information with employees falls short of the full concept of a program which is essential in both industrial relations and democratic processes. The attitude of willingness on which a sound and lasting program can be built is an expression of the genius of free enterprise.

In the old free enterprise unit of six or seven men, working for and with the boss, there was no problem of sharing information. The men who worked for wages and the boss who worked for profits understood each other. They thought alike about the American way, because they had the same facts on which to build their thinking. In such a unit, the boss never thought of any deliberate plan to share information with employees. Emphatically, he never thought of keeping any of it away from them.

That whole-hearted co-operation of the man who works for wages, co-operation based on his personal knowledge of the enterprise and his place in it, is tragically rare in the big industrial enterprise of today. In the absence of this understanding co-operation, industry has used a series of substitutes. Organization, supervision, and scientific management have established and enforced a necessary tempo of performance. Specialization of tasks has not only reduced the requirements of skills but has made easier the objective measurement of production. Automatic precision machinery, laboratory tests, and standard specifications have accomplished the requirements of quality. Scientific wage scales, or collective bargaining, have induced the wage earner to sell his time. Statements of policy, slogans, personnel departments, and welfare and medical work have been substituted for the old personal contact with the boss.

But in the change from the local wagon shop to Colossal Motors, from the village gristmill to Mammoth Foods, from the cabinet shop at Smith's Corners to the furniture factory in Grand Rapids, we have lost the old sharing of information and understanding. With it we lost the only internal force which impels a wage earner to give his best to the enterprise of which he is a part. We lost even the ability to demonstrate that he is a part of the enterprise and that the enterprise is a part of him and his life. And, finally, we lost the attitude on the part of the employer which enabled him to permit every fellow worker to know the business facts as a normal and personal right.

Millions of workers today do not understand, do not believe, that the establishments for which they work have an interest identical with their own. Thousands of employers have failed to see that the co-operation they want from workers must be paid for in more than money wages, that it must be paid for in the sure and open knowledge that the prosperity and continuity of the enterprise mean the prosperity and security of the wage-earning member of the team.

Many of us have preached the doctrine that the interest of the employer and employee are one and the same. But few of us have given to the employee the information which would enable him to judge for himself. Many of us have appealed for the loyalty of the wage earner to the enterprise which pays his wages. But few of us have shared with him the facts which would produce what we need more than "loyalty"—the enlightened, unceasing determination to put his best into the enterprise because he sees the sure result of returns to himself in prosperity and security.

The negative, "reluctant," willingness to share information with employees because they may get it anyway is hardly vigorous enough to stand comparison with the aggressive force of the American free-enterprise system.

The "paternalistic" willingness to share information with employees as part of the duty inherent in our positions as employers and leaders is hardly consistent with a practical recognition of what we mean by democracy.

The "propagandist" willingness is more smart than wise.

But there is an aggressive willingness to share information with employees which has a foundation both deeper and more practical. It reaches deep into the soil of democracy, being rooted in the recognition that John Jones, wage-earning employee, is a sacred human individual. His best achievement as a worker must be voluntary; it must be reached in co-operation with all the other independent personalities grouped into the enterprise of which he is a part. To gain satisfactory performance merely by bribing him with wages and privileges, or by threatening him vaguely with unemployment, is to repudiate the sacredness of his personality. To share with him the knowledge which should enable him to reason his way to willing co-operation is to treat his personality with the respect he deserves.

This aggressive willingness to share information with employees is practical because, honestly and wisely followed through, it will induce a constructive co-operation which cannot be bought or forced. It demands an enterprise which will through the years provide income and security for the employee who invests his life in it and which will at the same time make his life significant. Given an enterprise so planned and managed, the fullest knowledge about it will bring to any thinking employee an interest in his work, his job, *his* enterprise, such as no other influence can produce.

Being practical and frankly, honestly, practical: If we want *our* employing enterprise to succeed and survive, we shall actively desire *our* employees to have information which will justify them in putting their best into the enterprise. If we want our American system of free enterprise to survive, we shall aggressively desire *all* employees to have information about, and an understanding self-interest in, its preservation.

V

WHAT INFORMATION?

In the development of the newer attitude toward sharing information with employees, management representatives have spent long hours in discussing the related problems of what, when, and how. It has been my privilege to sit in on dozens of such discussions. This chapter reflects the thinking of most of these employers, as they have actually expressed themselves, on the "what" of this compound question. It reports what they said on the subject of the information they want their employees to have; also on the information, if any, which some of them are unwilling to give to employees.

These employers talked both in terms of general classes of information and in terms of definite items. Among general classes, they talked of such subjects as the company's finances, its place in the industry, and the regional and national problems of the industry as a whole. Among definite items they mentioned such things as the president's salary, the competitor's newly patented improvement, and last year's taxes.

Employers in one industry have private reasons for hoping their employees will not get certain information—information which employers in another industry are constantly trying to give to their employees. For example, almost all manufacturers want their employees to have a knowledge of the raw materials entering into their products. A manufacturer of veneer panels wanted his employees to know the sources of his raw materials—spruce from Oregon, maple from Vermont, mahogany from Africa, gum woods from Guatemala and the Philippines, stains from a dozen sources, plastic binders from others. But a manufacturer of certain proprietary drugs was shocked at the very idea! Perhaps the materials were inexpensive compared to the sale price of the product. Perhaps the ingredients represented a secret formula, the loss of which would endanger the whole enterprise.

It is relatively easy to list a dozen classes of information which most employers would agree are those which employees should have. The disagreements appear when we attempt to discuss the definite items. The differences even appear when we try to decide the scope of a given class of facts. To know whether we agree or not, we must name things so that we both have the same general picture.

A score of classes of information may be named by employers as those concerning which, with certain limitations and reservations, they sincerely want to share information with employees. The classes on which they generally agree include the following:

Company finances
Company personnel and organization
Company history
Labor policies
Company position in its own industry
Company products and their uses
Expansion plans
Sales and order prospects
Research activities
Industry outlook
Taxation

The fact that these classes or fields of information are stated in general language is the reason they are approved in general by most employers. But when any one of these broad fields is subjected to closer survey, limitations and reservations begin to be named. The honest opinions as to the propriety and need of sharing this or that class of information with employees show increasing differences as the field in question is divided and subdivided. Because these differences of attitude are sincere and practical, we record them, and try to fit them into the pattern of a modern and progressive effort to build understanding by sharing information with employees.

Almost without disagreement, employers will say they

want their employees to have information about the company's finances. To provoke any serious disagreement, one must explore and map the field in considerable detail. Here is a possible map of the field called "Company finances" on such a scale as will show its significant parts:

COMPANY FINANCES

A. Company Investment
  1. Nature of properties
  2. Source of funds
    a) Equity or venture capital
    b) Funded debt
    c) Current debt
  3. Distribution of ownership
  4. Investment per employee
  5. Surplus and reserves; what they are for, where the money is

B. Company Profits
  1. Total amount of profits
  2. Profit per dollar invested
  3. Profit per unit of product or service
  4. Profit per dollar of wages
  5. Profit per employee
  6. Profit compared with other years
  7. Profit retained for improvements, etc.

C. Company Costs
  1. Raw Materials
    a) Nature
    b) Source
    c) Quantities
    d) Costs; danger of waste
  2. Wages and salaries
    a) Ratio to other costs
    b) Salaries of officers
    c) Wage rates compared with others in industry or locality
  3. Taxes
    a) Relation to wages
    b) Taxes per employee; theoretical number of employees whose work goes entirely to taxes

- *c*) Relation to net profits
- *d*) Relation to dividends
- *e*) Taxes per share of stock
- *f*) Relative taxes from year to year
- *g*) Social security taxes

4. Depreciation, depletion, and obsolescence
   - *a*) What they mean
   - *b*) What becomes of reserves; why they are not kept in cash
   - *c*) Job protection by rehabilitation and modernizing of plant

D. Working Capital
1. Definition, uses, and needs
2. "Tied-up" working capital, paid out in advance of sales or realization
3. Typical demands for materials, supplies, payrolls

The average reader can construct a longer and more significant list. One common standard will apply to the lists which any of us might compile: Thinking as employers, we should list the kinds of information which have enabled us to comprehend the problems of our business. We therefore identify them as the kinds of information which will enable employees to understand the enterprise and their part in it.

This is sound and honest, as far as it goes. It must go farther. Our own experience is not a true guide as to what information will enable the employee to understand his relation to the business. The information which will do this is the information which answers his own questions. We must plan to share with him the information which he wants to get.

We must do so at first because that is the only information he will accept. This is an immediate but temporary fact. As his first desires for information are met, additional questions and interests will be stimulated. But we must, at first and always, give him the information *he* wants, because there will be no understanding until *his* questions are answered, *his* doubts and suspicions cleared away.

What does he want to know?

If the reader will think as a wage earner, he can construct a list of things which he would want to know. He can do this particularly well if his own days as a wage earner are not too far behind or if his present contact with wage earners is close and friendly.

Items for this list will come from his memories of questions he tried to ask of the older employees when he himself was new and from questions the newer employees have asked him now that he is one of the veterans. Other items will be suggested by questions the working supervisors have brought to higher executives of the business—questions which workers have presented to their supervisors and which the supervisors were not fully prepared to answer.

Still others will relate to rumors which have blossomed on the "grapevine," chance comments in casual conversations, and comments which reflect unfortunate misconceptions of many phases of the business. These chance expressions of mistaken ideas are priceless indications of the subject matter on which employees both need and want information. The fact that employees have heard, remembered, and repeated a wrong report is evidence that the subject involved is one in which they are interested.

Whatever the source of our ideas of what employees want to know, a careful listing of that supposedly desired information will produce something quite different in form from our own list of the classes of information we hope to share with employees.

If we succeed reasonably in reflecting the attitude of the employee mind, we shall not produce a list of classes of information. We shall not use words which are general or which are broadly inclusive. We shall not be able to list "company personnel" as something about which employees want information; but we are likely to remember several remarks or questions indicating that some employees want to know where that new assistant manager came from and how he got the job. We cannot intelligently assume that employees are interested in the broad subject of wages as an element in operating costs, but we can recall very clearly that John Brown wanted to know why his job pays only $32 a week while the same job at the Jones Corporation pays $38. There is no foundation for the belief that employees are interested in the principles or general ratios of profits; but there is plenty of reason to know that some of them at least are interested in the newspaper story that our business reported a profit of a million dollars for a certain period.

Employee questions and employee interests in information about the business are very specific, very practical, and naturally so. We cannot emphasize too strongly that men and women who work for wages are realists. Their wages must purchase and pay for real things: not only for food in general, but milk, bread, butter, eggs, and hamburger; not for clothes in general, but for a new dress for the wife, new shoes for Johnnie, and new overalls in which to work.

Obviously we can take the employer's list of general subjects on which he desires to share information with employees and break it down, analyze it, subdivide it, until it reflects specific items. And by the same process we can take the specific items on which we know employees want information, assemble and classify them, and find that they form general subject groups. But instead of finding that the two operations have represented merely the opposite courses along the same road, we shall experience some interesting conflicts in our thinking.

We may start, from the employer attitude, with a conviction that it would be a good thing if our employees knew more about the general subject of the investment in our business, how many stockholders own the business, and the fact that over 90 per cent of them own less than a hundred shares each. But it seems to us impertinent if an employee wants to know how many shares Reginald Rubber owns, if Reginald happens to be myself, or yourself.

We have agreed in the abstract that employees should know more about company costs. But we may not identify this conclusion with the unreasonable desire of the salesgirls to know the real cost of the hairbrush which sells for $3.00 and on which their sales commission is only eighteen cents.

We may be fully convinced that information about the company research program should be shared with employees. We may feel that this will help them to understand how their long-range employment security is identified with expenditures and efforts looking toward new and improved products, processes, or services. But it does not follow that we are willing, or should be willing, to answer the specific question as to what methods have already been discarded as unsuccessful in the effort to prevent the shine which develops on our new staple fiber cloth when it is used as material for men's suits. Nor does it follow that we can answer whether our laboratory is able to match our competitor's new spray method for applying lip rouge.

The point to be considered is not whether all the questions asked or likely to be asked by employees are pertinent, constructive, or useful. The point is that we must begin our whole thinking by realizing, as nearly as we can, what questions are in the minds of employees. We must be as realistic about our problem as they are about theirs. If we believe that the desired relationship of understanding can be aided by sharing information with employees, we must face the fact that we cannot successfully convey any information to them without meeting these questions which are in their minds. If we can find out what they want to know, we have a priceless opening for our program. But if we ignore, evade, or generalize instead of specifically meeting their questions, we have supplied material for building higher the wall of misunderstanding.

Some employers have provided question boxes in which employees are invited to deposit questions they want answered about the business. To the best of my knowledge there is little to recommend this as a method of deciding what information to share with employees. The channel is an artificial one, not a natural part of the relationship. It seems to suggest that employees cannot ask questions, man to man, of their immediate supervisors. But the results have at times been interesting. Of course, there has been a certain amount of childish misuse of the invitation. Besides reasonable and unreasonable questions, some such boxes have yielded anonymous screeds commenting on the appearance, character, attitude, and ancestry of an unpopular foreman, upon the judgment of the president in buying a new yacht instead of raising wages, and upon the preference of the writer for full-time work instead of a turkey at Christmas. But they have yielded, for a short time, some honest reflections of employee interest, as well as some hopelessly impertinent questions.

Other employers, singly or in groups, have engaged the services of expert research organizations to make surveys of employee interest in information about the business. When well planned and executed, such surveys have contributed greatly to wise programs by employers for meeting the desires of employees for business facts.

Whatever mechanism may be used to answer the question of what information to share with employees, certain premises will eventually be accepted. Among others, these will probably be commonly included:

1. The information must match up with questions in the mind of the employee; and the information given can purposefully stimulate other questions.
2. No field of information can be excluded if it will help to promote understanding of the business and the employee's relation to it.
3. Not all the questions raised can or should be answered;

but a question which is impertinent or antagonistic should not be ignored, nor a question which would reveal confidential facts capable of misuse. In such cases, the author of the question has presented a valuable opportunity for an explanation of why the specific information is not of use to him or may be dangerous to his long-range interests if released.

There are some types of information which management should share with employees but which in the interest of both employer and employee should not be broadcast to the world. Experience has shown that such information can sometimes actually be protected by sharing it with employees rather than by an excess effort at secrecy. Given the necessary previous demonstration of the willingness of management to share information with them, employees are likely to guard the facts which should be guarded. There will be "leaks" at times; not every employee will have the ethics or the judgment to keep some news which is "too good to keep." But disclosures of this kind are likely to be less frequent and less harmful than those which are carried over the "grapevine" when employees themselves are not trusted with the correct information.

The relationship wherein employees know that they can have information about the business and, at the same time, that they themselves will be hurt if that information "gets out," is a far milepost on the road to understanding. When that relationship has been achieved, employees have an instinctive sense of identity with the enterprise. Facts about it are theirs. Disclosure of some of these facts would hurt the business and therefore hurt the employees' own interests. This sense of identity of interest is the essence of understanding. Therefore, if sharing with employees the information which competitors should not have will hasten the creation of this sense, such sharing is worth some risk of premature disclosure.

One instance was related to me by a friend which shows the long-range value of an occasional "leak." The employer in this case was a manufacturer of a well-known product sold at retail in every city in competition with a like product from many other makers, and bought by the average employee. Let us say that it was an everyday shirt. This manufacturer felt the necessity of enlisting employee help to reduce waste, not merely by being careful but also by contributing thought. Through a channel already well established he frankly revealed to employees the actual detail of the direct cost of this particular style. They saw a direct finished cost of 87 cents against a retail price of $1.50, but he casually revealed some of the other elements—overhead, taxes, discounts to dealers, and so on. The important point was that the average waste per shirt was nearly four cents, as against one cent on most styles. Employee co-operation was prompt. Care was intensified, and two or three good suggestions helped to improve the method and the process. The final saving in cost was actually more than four cents of waste.

But, in the meantime, a local newspaper carried an article headed "Who Gets the 63 Cents?" The article presented the detail of the 87 cents of factory cost, and implied that either the manufacturer or the retailer was profiteering! At this point the result was so unfortunate that it seemed to outweigh by far the saving of four or five cents in manufacturing costs. However, the most valuable results were still to come. The employees themselves moved into the publicity. Along one line of attack, they induced the publisher to print additional facts which gave his readers an education in such subjects as distribution costs, overhead, and taxes. Along another line they traced his source of information into their own ranks, and gave their fellow worker a constructive lesson in the protection of his interests and theirs.

With commendable wisdom, this employer continued to maintain the same open channel for sharing information with his employees, just as frankly as before. If I should identify either his name or the product he really makes, most of my readers would recognize a widespread enterprise with tens of thousands of workers in a disturbed industry, but an enterprise which is a model of constructive relations with employees and free from the labor troubles which beset most of its competitors. This understanding has grown from many seeds. One is sharing information with employees with the positive expectation that when necessary they will protect the information because it, too, is part of their enterprise!

When we try to build understanding by sharing information with employees, we are demonstrating that we trust them, in the faith that they will come to trust us and each other. If we are too highly selective as to the kinds of information we share with them, we shall fail this time, and for a long time to come, in making measurable progress toward the understanding our industrial enterprise needs.

In the following chapters, we discuss briefly two specific classes of information which we can profitably share with employees, and one which we should religiously avoid. The three subjects are presented merely as samples. It is a temptation to write similar chapters on such subjects as costs, sales, profits, research, raw-material supplies, and personalities. Each of these or of a dozen other subjects deserves discussion. Perhaps someone will write a book about each of them, viewed as a subject on which information may be shared with employees. Without apology, the next three chapters touch on only three selected sample subjects.

VI

INFORMATION ABOUT THE INVESTMENT

Information about the investment covers a wide scope. The first reaction of employers to the thought of sharing that kind of information with employees is almost always negative. Such information still has a somewhat sacred atmosphere. Such information is technical, or at least complicated. Such information is dry, factual, statistical; it has no appeal to such people as employees.

The sacred atmosphere has been largely dispelled by enforced publication, at least in the case of corporations, with the result that most significant facts about company capital are available to anyone who desires to obtain them. And this enforced publicity was aimed at bad practices by some corporate managements. With such an origin, it is only natural that publicity laws and regulations and their administration are unfriendly to corporate management. Because of the sins of some, sins actual but exaggerated or sometimes merely suspected, all management has been subjected to suspicion.

But while it is clear that the great majority of men in management never were guilty of the alleged sins of commission, they may have been guilty of a sin of omission. They may have failed to share information regarding company capital, its sources and its uses, first with those who have supplied the venture with capital, and, second, with those who stake their working lives on the soundness of the capital structure and the efficiency of the use of that capital.

If the elimination of the air of sacredness—and secrecy—around the story of company investment leads to a more generous sharing of the story with stockholders and employees alike, the result may be a sounder and healthier setting for the free-enterprise system. It may avoid future indiscriminate legislation.

Perhaps information about company investment has been technical or complicated in its expression rather than in its substance. Of course, the facts about the five-step holding-company structure were complicated, perhaps purposely complicated. No one could clearly describe such facts to stockholders or to anyone else; and perhaps no one seriously tried. But the investment story of any ordinary enterprise can be reduced to simple units: The enterprise needed certain things in advance of any income from its customers. Some persons supplied the money for these needs. They either supplied it subject to all the risk—venture capital—or they supplied it with some assurance against the risk—loan capital. Some of it may have come from sellers who extended temporary credit to the new enterprise for things it needed. Such money, whether venture capital, loan capital, or credit, was used to acquire ground, buildings, raw material, and tools, to make known the service or product to possible customers, and to pay wages until money began to come in from customers.

Those are the basic, simple facts about the capital investment of any enterprise. They are the everyday translation of one portion of the highly technical document called the balance sheet.

Yes, the information is dry, factual, statistical. So are mortality rates, birth rates, and school statistics. All are in the same class if we do not see the realities behind the fact-and-figure symbols. The infant mortality rate expresses the number of infant deaths per 100,000 live-born babies. Is that dry, factual, statistical? Not to the Smiths who are expecting a baby next month; not to the Joneses who have the twins now six months old; above all, not to the Browns whose three-months-old son died last week. And every figure added and divided to produce the symbol called "rate of infant mortality" was the symbol of a real baby born to real parents!

School statistics—registration, age groups, average daily attendance, retardation, achievement quotients, cost per pupil—these are dry, factual, statistical. But every unit, figure, or symbol is alive and vibrant! Behind every digit in the tables is the black-eyed girl from our house, the red-headed boy across the street.

One of the best jobs I ever knew of making "company investment" take on life meaning is done by a manager of a small plant employing about five hundred. This manager systematically plans to see each new employee soon after he joins the organization. He plans the conversation so that he can ask the new employee why he prefers to work for wages rather than for himself. Of course, the answer is almost always "I have no capital. You gotta have capital to go in business for yourself."

Wisely and slowly this manager leads to recognition of the fact that capital is no less necessary if the man is to work for wages. He points out the visible, physical things which had to be provided before he, or anyone else, could work for wages in that plant—the purchase of the land, the buildings, spur tracks, the heavy equipment, machines, and tools. He casually jots down figures as he goes along, mentions the total dollars, the number of workers; and he and the employee together discover that the physical plant represents $22,000 per worker!

They follow through, together, the steps of deciding that this investment, this capital, must be paid some rent or wages; they agree that 6 per cent is fair. They also agree that the part of the investment which wears out must be paid off or replaced; so they get acquainted with depreciation. They reach a point where they decide that each employee must produce gross earnings of some $2,000 a year, just to pay for the investment he uses, before he can earn any wages for himself!

Do you think that figures on company investment are going to be merely dry and factual to an employee who has been introduced to them in this way? There is an almost unlimited opportunity to dramatize facts about company investment merely in this one method of treatment—investment per worker. There is the comparison of investment per worker in our industry and in other industries. In the plant mentioned above, the $22,000 per worker compares with an average of less than $5,000 in United States manufacturing as a whole. Perhaps the sequence is that the employee will feel some pride and responsibility for having such a high relative investment behind his job.

Perhaps in another plant the investment per worker is below the average, perhaps only $2,000 per employee. Probably this will lead to the knowledge that wages represent a much higher proportion of cost in that plant than in the average plant. This opens a whole new field of information and interest—the field of costs and their control by mutual effort.

Soon after they are introduced in any intelligent way to the subject of investment some employees will "open up" on the unfair distribution of profits: capital gets too much, labor too little. One corporation executive found his way into such a conversation by accident. He found a wise channel into which to direct the talk; now he seeks opportunity for such discussions.

The accidental first experience involved a committee of three employees who had come in to talk about something else. The talk drifted up to a remark by one of them that he hoped to see the day when labor would get a fairer share. The executive agreed in principle, but remarked that the decision of what was a fair share for capital was difficult; the return must be enough to cover some risk, enough to compete with other investment opportunities, or funds could not be obtained when needed for expansion or replacement.

The outspoken employee agreed that all this was true, but insisted there was a limit to the return capital should expect. Said the executive: "Jim, what do you think would be a fair return for capital invested in a business like ours?" "Well, I'd say 8 per cent."

"Do you mean 8 per cent a year, as an average over the years?" "Yes," said Jim.

The executive then took out some of his private papers, enough to show the prices at which he had bought his present stock. They then added up all the dividends received on the stock, and, figuring together, line by line, reached the discovery that the average for the whole time was 3 per cent a year.

There is a curious unanimity among employees in setting 8 per cent as the fair return on invested capital. It will be the announced opinion of most of them in most industries if the casual tests of recent years are typical. There is almost equal unanimity of failure among American industrial enterprises to pay this return to their stockholders, or to common and preferred stockholders combined, or to stockholders and bondholders combined, over any consecutive period of ten, fifteen, or twenty years.

From this point, employer and employee have other roads of discussion open to them. One follows easily to the price at which someone else bought his stock. Perhaps he paid only $10 a share and his average per cent of return has been higher than mine, based on my average purchase price of $15. With that, we can move fearlessly and gladly into the reasons why prices of the stock rise and fall, how investors feel about our business compared with others, and—a most helpful channel in most enterprises—how much of the investment has remained in the hands of the same owners year after year. There is a healthy achievement in getting employees to see that their company is looked upon as an investment, not as a speculation. This helps to banish the ghost of Wall Street!

Another tangent is suggested—who the investors really

are. How many stockholders are there? What is their average investment? How many own a hundred shares or less? Are many of them employees or former employees? Who are the stockholders—bankers, widows, workers, institutions?

Wisely approached, there are few subjects on which information will be more readily received by employees than the subject of company investment. Fairly considered, there are few subjects on which they have a greater right to receive information. There are few subjects which more naturally open channels of inquiry and interest in other subjects—costs, taxes, reserves, sales, research—every factor which affects investment security *and thereby affects employment security*.

Examples have been given of natural conversational opportunities to share such information with employees. All other techniques are applicable in this field. But here it is particularly evident that natural conversation is the ideal method. Natural conversation need not be accidental. It may be induced in a hundred ways.

When a corporation supplies its annual statement to employees, the corporation officers cannot believe—and should not hope—that satisfactory and complete knowledge of company finances, operations, progress, and prospects have thereby been given to employees. With all the improvement in form and content of corporation reports in recent years, none has yet been devised to present a full picture—a still picture of dated condition and a moving picture of period activities.

But the corporation officers can hope for a greater success. If the financial report brings questions from a few employees, a great result has been achieved. If one employee in ten voices some question prompted by some item in the report, the officers and management can give thanks without measure.

Some of those questions will naturally concern the company investment, and to them responses should be ready at every point in the organization where the questions are likely to be presented. Most of all, the foreman or supervisor, as the most likely target of the questions, must be equipped to respond.

Like the annual statement, any other technique of sharing information can be planned to elicit questions about some phase of company investment. Bulletin-board notices, newspaper items, direct letters, house-organ articles—any of these can create interest and stimulate questions about company investment. It requires skill, patience, and sincerity to plan the use of these media to prompt these questions. It requires greater skill and planning, earlier and longer, to have the right responses ready, at the right place, to meet these questions.

VII

INFORMATION ABOUT THE WORK

No matter what may be the detail under immediate consideration in the larger problem of achieving a relationship of understanding with employees, we may well return to the old industrial unit in which this understanding was so generally present. We have pictured such a unit in a furniture and cabinet shop where six or seven "hired hands" and the boss worked together.

Understanding was there, based on knowledge. The knowledge, as always, was the product of a complete sharing of information. The employees, the six or seven who worked for wages, knew all the problems of the boss. Knowing the problems, they recognized them as their own as well as his. They shared his interest in raw-material sources and costs, manufacturing costs, selling costs, selling prices, collections, customer satisfaction, future orders. The growth of the modern industrial enterprise has cut off the natural contacts through which they had this information and, in most cases, has provided no substitute.

One phase of the knowledge which workers lost in this evolution has an importance only recently recognized by most of us, knowledge of the significance of the particular work which each employee performs. The specialization of work was an essential factor in the evolution of modern industry. The level on which we live could not have been attained, and cannot continue to be occupied today, without this specialization. Great aggregations of capital, gigantic manufacturing plants, supplies of electric power, automatic machines and machine tools, standard models, assembly-line methods, and all the other factors of mass production could never have given us the abundance of material things at low cost which are characteristic of our American living without the specialization of labor.

The American worker has gained in a material way by this evolution. Without mass production and its coincident specialization of labor, the average worker could not own an automobile, a radio, an electric washer. These and a thousand other factors of physical comfort could never have been produced and distributed at prices within the reach of most wage earners.

But against these gains there must be listed the loss of the worker's personal view of the results of his workmanship. This is a loss to him and to all of us. In the old furniture and cabinet shop, each worker saw the finished job. He saw his workmanship combined with that of his fellows to make the perfect whole. We can imagine the day when the dining-room "suit" of table and six chairs was ready for delivery. Seven men and the boss, with equal concern and equal pride, looked it over. Each was alert to find any imperfection in the finished product. One recalled what a tricky job it was to match the grain in the table top. Another mentioned the hard time they had had getting that carving just right, on the chair backs. Another remembered the days of work that went for nothing when the first table top warped. They all talked about how hard it had been to satisfy the customer as to shade of stain and softness of finish.

Of course, few men who work for wages today could have the dining-room furniture they have in their own homes if it were still made under those conditions. To bring such furniture within reach of the purse of the millions, great factories have been built. They are equipped with costly semiautomatic machinery. Their hundreds or thousands of workers have taken on highly specialized repetitive tasks. One spends his time at a lathe, turning out eighteen hundred identical chair rungs every day. He may not know whether the birch he uses will leave the factory with a walnut, a mahogany, or a bleached finish. Another does nothing all day long but produce dowels or pegs. Another makes the soft-wood bases for table tops, to which others will add the veneer. Another has charge of a planer, or a shaper which makes the seats for chairs.

Of course, all this must be so if we are to have the abundance of things at the costs we can pay. But until the sense of accomplishment is restored to the specialized worker, we are courting the social disaster of a new type of peasant psychology. As far as his work is concerned, every mass-production worker is almost condemned to the lack of vision without which "the people perish."

It is true that specialization and mass production have brought the worker other chances to grow and acquire vision. The less able ones have been given semiskilled tasks which have made their earnings and purchasing power greater than those of the most skilled craftsmen of the last generation. All have gained abundant leisure to enjoy the comforts of the mass-production economy: the automobile and the good roads, the movie, the radio, the electrified household, and the low-cost books and magazines are blessings to be enjoyed in this added leisure time. But our concern is not only with the mental growth and attitude off the job. We have a self-interest in the attitude on the job, and our methods have not fully served our own best interest. We are deeply concerned over the way our city and state are governed, by the votes of our fellow citizens who work for wages. But we are more immediately concerned over the question whether or not the wages we pay are enlisting the minds as well as the hands of these same fellow workers.

If your job is to stand at Position 17 on the conveyor line, and put Bolt 113-A into Hole 113 all day long, how much of your mental ability do you give to the job? And what can we do about it, without tearing out the conveyor and going back to the process of having each man do a complete-cycle job?

A simple story has come down to us from the days when work itself was simpler than it is today. It probably is a narration of true facts. It certainly is a revelation of true thoughts.

At the scene of a large construction job, a number of men with chisels and mallets were working on blocks of granite. There was no Sidewalk Superintendents Club then, not even a board fence to provide knotholes. So the curious observer walked close to the workmen.

To the first one he said, "May I ask what you are making?" The answer was "Six dollars a day, and it's none too much for this back-breaking job if you want to know."

Moving on, he asked another workman, working on another block of granite, the same question: "What are you making?" Although the material and the operation were the same, the answer was different: "I'm making a flat face on the front of this block of stone."

To still a third man he put the question, a man doing the same work on another identical block of granite. "What are you making?" But an answer so different: "I'm helping to make the facing for the new Cathedral. If you want to see what it's going to look like, there's a picture of it over there in the Superintendent's shack. That's what I'm helping to make."

For years we have told or heard this story and thought of it as revealing the differences in attitudes of men toward their jobs. It does reveal or illustrate these differences but it also turns our thoughts to another truth: Someone had taken the trouble to tell that third man, in such a way that he took it into his life, about the cathedral that was to be. Each of those men was "making" six dollars a day; each was "making" a flat face on the front of a block of stone; each was helping to "make" the facing for the new cathedral. But only the third man knew in a meaningful way the one fact which transformed the unpleasant granite dust and the blistered hands into something of future beauty; the one fact which related the daily wage and the blocks of stone to the significance of the structure rising to serve the believers of that faith through uncounted years. By accident, by instinct, or by wisdom, someone had made Worker Number Three a conscious part of the life of his city, a conscious contributor to the progress of his own people. Somehow I wish I might have been the one to give such a vision and realization to a fellow worker.

Another story which is literally true comes from a real furniture factory. A pattern of bedroom furniture which carried a painted floral decoration was being produced. As an example of efficient specialization, four stencils were cut, for the four colors included in the design. One group of workers received the headboards and applied the first color, through the first stencil. Next day the same headboards, with that paint dried, reached another group of workers, each of whom spent his day applying the second color through the second stencil. And so to the third and fourth or final color, and slight retouching by a fifth worker. The plan of specialization was obviously more efficient than the employment of a sufficient number of near-artists, each of whom could paint the whole picture. But there was evidence of depression, fatigue, boredom, lack of interest.

Simple, straight thinking found an answer. As each new model or design was put into production, the whole group of stencilers were taken to a display room and shown the completed model before their stenciling task began. Each was given a color sketch of the completed design to which his stencil job was to be a contribution. The job of putting on the first color through the first stencil became alive. It became one step in creating a picture which the worker felt was partly his achievement.

The same idea was carried through that entire factory. Each finished product was introduced to each worker who made a contribution to it. The insignificant, boresome task which he blindly repeated, hour after hour, became a significant step in a significant process, of which he had seen the end result.

In hundreds of mass-production processes, the same principle has found a place. But the expression of this principle in the larger program of sharing information with employees has only begun. For besides the visual inspection of the completed article toward which his special job contributes, the average worker can receive information in many other ways, information which will give meaning to his daily work.

There is a wide range of knowledge about the materials with which he works. In the furniture plant, or any other wood products industry, he will "eat up" facts about the wood sources. He can be given information about the forest locations, pictures of trees and logging, preliminary sawmill operations, selection, grading, transportation, seasoning, reaction to stains, and finishes. If he is working with petroleum, he will enjoy knowing the stories of exploration, wild-cat drilling, reserves, international rivalries, military uses, and native population in oil-field areas. If he works in a clothing factory, he will be spontaneously interested in the sources of imported and domestic cloths, the struggle to replace the missing imports with American fabrics, the blending of Scotch, American, and Australian wools, the manner of life of Australian sheep raisers, the tariff problems, the romance of the substitute "staple fiber" made from rayon, and the gradual displacement of silk by rayon in the lining satins.

There is an equally wide field of knowledge about the processes themselves—knowledge which is perhaps more intimately connected with his own work. He will "tune in" and receive any information we can offer about what has been done before the process reaches his task. He will take on new interest from knowing that ten men or a hundred men have each done some part of a job before the headboard of the bed reaches him for the application of the first stencil. He can better understand his own task, the other worker's task, and the manager's task, if he is shown why some surfaces take the paint more easily than others, why some special fillers have been used, and how they were applied.

Another vision is opened up by facts concerning his work in its relation to the use of the finished product. Knowledge that the article is for export to South Africa may give meaning to the instructions he has just received which otherwise did not make sense.

The evolution of his own particular task can be so revealed as to create new interest in life for him. If he is operating an automatic machine which with astonishing rapidity "carves" the claw feet on chair legs, there are volumes of history on the art of wood carving to tell him the ancestry of his semiskilled task. From these histories can be digested a story of the evolution of modern machine carving. Made available in an attractive way, such a brief history will create an interest in a widening knowledge of present-day wood carving. The worker may develop a hobby of collecting facts about the persistence of hand carving today. From such a simple stimulation, the imagination of a worker has more than once produced an inventive suggestion to enable the semiautomatic machine to do a more delicate and beautiful job, possessing one more characteristic of the art of the handcraft worker.

In some modern industrial plants where labor tasks are highly specialized and subdivided, an effort is made to reveal the progress of the particular equipment on which the workers operate. It is not difficult to picture an increased interest in such a monotonous task as tending a modern spinning jenny, if each machine attendant has an opportunity to see frequently a working model of the first spinning jenny.

The evolution of the equipment is as interesting a subject as the history of the process or the product.

Information about the work methods in competitive plants usually receives a willing hearing. Displays of samples of competitive products, arranged so that workers on similar products can see them, will often attract surprising interest. Workers in secondary manufacturing plants, converting the products of other factories, show ready interest in any form of information about the manufacturing processes which provide them with the materials for their own work.

But the limited interest of workers in their own work is an amazing indication of the extent to which we have allowed the significance of the modern specialized task to be obscured. One company whose management prides itself on its modern practices in employee relations recently scheduled an "open house," during which visitors were specially invited to see the work in progress. One of the shocking surprises was the number of employees who used their own time off work to go through the plant as visitors. They wanted to see the processes related to their own. One employee who had worked for twelve years on a process of converting a product made in one section of the mill and who went through as a visitor explained that he had always wanted to see the basic manufacture of the product on which he worked but had never had the chance before!

The interest of employees in their own work can sometimes be awakened with surprising ease. Most of the readers will recall the recent story of an experiment in research which accomplished this result merely by explanation of the studies to the workers concerned. Experiments were made first with increased light and then with decreased light for one group and with unchanged light for another group; also with rearrangement of parts for assembly, with shorter hours and longer hours, added rest periods, and many other theoretical improvements. The experiments included reversals of all improvements which had been made in facilities or working conditions. No matter what was done, the efficiency of the workers, as measured by output, was increased. So far no explanation has been found except that worker interest had been enlisted and stimulated by advance discussion of every change which was made and of the absence of change when that in itself was the factor of experiment. The task of every worker had been made important and significant in his own eyes.

The management of one other plant which maintained "open house" for visitors for the first time was prepared for reduced output during the visiting hours, owing to the distraction and general disruption of routine entailed. However, the program had been explained to every employee by his immediate line supervisor in such a way that there was general interest in "showing off" before both strangers and friends. Considerable expense was involved in the preparations and in the reception and guidance of visitors, yet efficiency for the period was so increased that the cost of the whole program was more than offset.

Another management, whose plant has some thousands of employees, maintains a school with a four-year course covering the industry in which the plant is engaged. The courses are not vocational, being intended not to improve the skill of the worker but rather to give him a comprehension of the industry. Included are studies of the history of the industry and of its varied sources of materials, its processes, marketing, organization, and economics. More than 50 per cent of the eligible employees have voluntarily enrolled in the school, on their own time, with no reward attached.

Almost all the conventional media for sharing information with employees can be applied to information about their work. Certain media, such as visual displays of materials, finished products, and products in process, are peculiarly applicable. Films, pictures, and descriptive texts are usable.

House organs, trade magazines, and even textbooks are given a good reception when they deal with the worker's work. But the work itself is assigned to him by his line supervisor. From this supervisor he receives instruction as to methods, quality and quantity of output, criticism for errors, commendation for good results. No other channel can do so much of the job of conveying information which will make the work interesting.

Line management has been so intent on getting the work done that it has devoted little time to conveying information about the work if it had no bearing on the immediate task. Management is now beginning to appreciate the factor of efficiency involved in sharing information which merely awakens interest. It has been shown that awakened interest means efficiency stemming from the release of mental energy. The tendency is to equip line supervisors to convey such information.

What is needed beyond this is the recognition that if such information can be shared so as to make routine jobs significant, the worker of tomorrow will be a spontaneously creative person, a safe trustee of the values of democracy and free enterprise, an understanding participant on the high level of living maintained by modern industry.

VIII

NOT POLITICS!

There are perfectly valid facts available at times of political campaigns which could be communicated within the strictest meaning of the words "sharing information with employees." If an employer has compiled and tabulated facts about taxes, public expenditures, graft, crime waves, or any specific deeds or misdeeds of a political administration, those facts are information. Obviously, a well-organized program for sharing information with employees can be utilized to convey such facts to employees.

This is not a treatise on the ethics of employers attempting to influence the politics and votes of their employees. Much could be said on both sides of that subject. Perhaps the most likely vice in such action would be assumed from the premise that employers are in a position to exert undue influence through imposing penalties on employees for refusal to accept their political advice. While this may have been true in some locations and relationships in some past generation, it has rarely been true in our day. But the theory persists.

There is a traditional, instinctive reaction against the use of any such power, or supposed power, to influence or control the political actions of the sovereign citizen. It is closely related to the prevalent reaction against government employees engaging in the rounding-up of votes. Much of the legislation supporting civil service and all of the philosophy of the Hatch Acts gives expression to this reaction; we are seeking to guarantee that government employees, holding power which is the power of government, shall not use that power to influence our personal votes. By the same reasoning or instinct, we feel that one who has the accidental status of employer should not apply pressure to the one universal right and privilege of the citizen—the ballot.

But entirely aside from the pure ethics, we can discuss the practical expediency of any attempt by employers to guide the political decisions of their employees as expressed at the ballot box. As an activity measured in terms of both short-term and long-term results, does it pay? Is it a wise practice for an employer to convey information to his employees which will indicate to them that he hopes or wishes that they vote this way or that?

Our whole interest in the program of sharing information with employees is with respect to understanding. Any information which will enable an employee to comprehend the underlying factors which affect his employment, earnings, and security, and which will enable him to see his stake in the enterprise and the free-enterprise system, has a place in our program. Will information about political officeholders and political administrations contribute to understanding, to more intelligent and co-operative relations between employers and employees?

Most employers who try to influence the politics or the votes of their employees are very sincere. They see that the long-range interests of the employees are actually endangered by the program of a certain candidate. They believe that his personality, eloquence, or specious arguments may appeal to the employee mind. They feel that it is their duty to exert a counter influence. The same sincerity usually marks their efforts to influence employees on measures as well as on men.

These employers make several mistakes. The first and most serious is the belief that they can influence the votes of their employees. The employer may know that his own knowledge is greater, his experience wider, his judgment better, than those of his employees. He feels that it is not only his right but his duty to give the employees the benefit of his knowledge, experience, and judgment.

He is thereby adding something new to his experience. And if his judgment is really good, one experiment will be enough. He will find that the effort is futile. It is even worse, because it creates or widens a gap between him and his fellow workers. They will generally reject his political advice, discount his judgment or his sincerity, and suspect his motives.

He makes another mistake, one common to many efforts toward sharing information with employees. That is the mistake of offering conclusions instead of facts. It is the mistake of trying to do the thinking for another man, instead of giving him access to fair and sufficient information on which to do his own thinking. This mistake is fundamental.

A third mistake is the belief that it is necessary to influence the political decisions of employees. By "influence" we mean persuade employees to vote for Jones instead of Smith or vote against a certain measure instead of for it. This implies that men who work for wages cannot reach correct or intelligent conclusions from known facts.

This attempt to tell employees how to vote—for that is what we are discussing—is basically unnecessary, in addition to being futile and dangerous. If we believe that the majority of the employees in our establishment, or in the city or the state, are likely to vote the wrong conclusions, we must not attribute that to their inability to reason out the right conclusions. In most cases, we should attribute it to the fact that they have not had access over a long-enough period to the necessary supply of facts from which right conclusions can be reasoned. If they have had the same facts as we, and have had as long a time to study them, and still have reached conclusions different from ours, it is always possible that their conclusions may even be right!

Besides being unnecessary, the effort to influence the political judgment of employees is contrary to our most important political principles. We have extended the vote to all adult citizens for the very reason that we are unwilling, ourselves, to submit to conclusions based on the judgment of a smaller portion of the people. We want the expression of the judgment of the greatest number so that the composite judgment will most surely be sound and in the interest of the greatest number. When the verdict of the majority disagrees with our desires, the cause may be one of three: the majority may have lacked some facts which we had; the judgment of the majority may have been wrong; or our judgment may have been wrong.

The hope for survival of our American way does not rest on any plan by which the better judgment of the few may dominate or influence the judgment of the many. It does lie in improving the judgment of the many. To achieve this we must share with them the experience of judging, even of judging wrongly, but of learning to judge more wisely through practice in judging. To achieve this, we must bend every effort toward the end that every citizen shall have adequate facts on which to practice in judging.

The information we need to share with employees must for practical reasons exclude those matters which bear directly on political campaigns. An American worker usually will not accept information when it is given with the obvious intention of influencing his vote—and that is exactly the attitude we want him to have as one of the fellow citizens by whom we ourselves are governed.

A member of the management staff of a large factory once said to a friend: "This election business puzzles me. I know that our employees believe in the management of this mill. They have engaged in arguments up town in which they asserted that our manager was the best in the industry. They are proud of his wisdom and ability. They know that he and his immediate associates were personally supporting Jones in the election. And in spite of their respect for our manager's brains and judgment, I'll bet that over 90 per cent of them voted against Jones."

The answer from his listener, who has spent years studying employee reactions, was this: "They respect your manager and you for good business judgment. They accept your support of Jones as an evidence of that business judgment. They don't argue with it; they assume that the election of Jones would have been good for the interests of management. For that very reason, they voted the opposite way, because they feel that the interests of management are fundamentally opposed to the interests of those who work for wages."

As a matter of fact, the attitude of the employees toward the management in that plant can be considered as correctly described by the first speaker. As a matter of logic, the explanation given by the second speaker can hardly be refuted. Accepting it as reasonably correct, we must follow to the obvious conclusion which was suggested earlier: It is useless, and worse, for management to take any steps to influence the votes of employees. The kind of information which management should share with employees has nothing to do with the relative merits of two candidates for public office; but it has everything to do with the disastrous idea that management and workers have basic interests which are opposed.

Any attempt to change the preconceived political opinions held by a majority of a group of employees merely adds strength to their belief that management is talking selfishly. Any attempt, close to election time, to convince employees that their interests are essentially the same as those of management is almost sure to be judged as an attempt to influence their votes.

Let us imagine ourselves in the midst of a political campaign. The dominant issue is free trade or reciprocity, versus high tariff. You and I are shingle manufacturers. Our plant has run half time during the past year. Shingle imports from Canada may have increased 150 per cent during that year. You and I can truthfully say to our employees: "You have lost 150 days of work this last year because of the reciprocity policy of this administration. Therefore, you should vote for the high-tariff party, get back your full-time jobs, and stop this flood of imported shingles." Will they believe us? Particularly, will they believe our conclusion as to how they should vote?

On general principles, probably not. Someone can persuade them that the reciprocity policy has actually increased total American exports by more than 100 per cent. Some local paper or politician can persuade them that we have not operated full time as part of a deliberate plot to create a depression and embarrass the administration.

During the recession of 1938, one of the more intelligent leaders of a conservative labor union, a man basically sincere and honest, said to me: "I've been reading everything I have seen on the subject, and I'm fully convinced that this recession was deliberately brought on by the big employers of the country. They expect to check the rising trend of wages for one thing, and they expect to influence the elections this fall by showing people that the policies of this administration have not been successful in restoring prosperity." Of course, when business improved, after the conservative swing in the elections of 1938, he and his associates were probably more firm in this opinion than ever. And the time before election, when he expressed himself as quoted above, was no time to begin a campaign to educate him.

Any facts which are obviously given to influence employee votes, or which are given during the heat of a political campaign, will not get a hearing. The same facts given under normal conditions, and directly related to their effects on the personal interests of the employee, will get a hearing. The extent to which these facts will lead to sound political judgment depends on the amount of opportunity employees have had to form their own political judgments on the basis of facts which have daily life significance.

Returning to this shingle mill of yours and mine, when orders fell off last year, we could have said to our employees: "We'll be finished with our last order a week from next Saturday. There is plenty of building going on, but some of our regular customers are buying Canadian shingles instead of ours. We can't blame a builder for that, because those shingles are just as good as ours and the price is $1.20 less. We don't know just how badly this will hurt us, but we know there will not be enough orders for full-time running for a while."

Such a statement might lead to questions about the total shingle imports, about relative transportation costs, relative wages, and other pertinent details. When the time came for political decisions, each employee would have this information in mind, received and accepted at a time when it had no immediate political implications. He might not reach the same political conclusions as you and I, for several reasons. For instance, he might have been receiving unexpected payments from his brother-in-law on an old debt, with the explanation that the brother-in-law was again working full time, and overtime in a tire factory because export business to Canada had doubled. Putting all his information together, our employee might decide that he believed in the over-all benefits of reciprocity.

But another possible form of understanding may have developed. Because he was given the information about our shingle business in relation to his own employment prospects, and without relation to his politics either by implication or by timing, he is more likely to feel free to seek more information from us. Many an employer has been asked where information can be obtained on total imports and exports during recent years. Our inquiring employee may want to know whether the increased exports of tires added enough employment in the United States to make up for the loss of employment in the shingle industry. Because we have told our story frankly, at the right time, without political inferences, he is likely to consider us and our foremen as reliable sources of other information.

IX

HOW?

We have taken as a major premise that management must take steps to promote understanding between employees and employers, and as a minor premise that sharing information with employees is one step toward understanding. We further recognize a wide field of information which can be shared with employees. The natural question to follow is how to share the information with them.

This must be more than a mere inquiry into the devices and methods which are physically available. It must be a critical study of available methods to determine which will best serve the ultimate purpose of creating understanding. The presentation of facts, even if the facts are accepted, will not promote understanding unless the manner of their presentation has been consistent with their substance and has been consistent with the actual relations already existing within the particular employing enterprise. Understanding between people cannot be achieved entirely on the basis of facts and statistics; it requires a revelation and a comprehension of attitudes, personalities, and character.

In later pages we shall view several of the conventional media which are available and which are widely used for sharing information with employees. Many or most of these media would be included in any survey in connection with a proposed advertising campaign. Many of them would be considered in connection with a political or educational campaign.

But our standards of judging the relative or absolute values of these media are distinctive, because our objective is fundamentally different. Our objective is a lasting and continuing attitude, not an early and conclusive action. We are not seeking to persuade employees to buy something or to do something specific. We are not even interested in causing them to know some particular fact or to think any specific thought.

No single item of information which we can share with employees will have any measurable effect in creating the understanding which is our goal. The sharing of enough information to form the basis of understanding is in itself a continuing task. The sharing of this information in ways that will stimulate interest in further information, and stimulate critical thinking, demands the choice of media which look in this direction and minimizes the need and value of spectacular statements which may be only temporarily effective in the sense of telling a fact and securing an immediate reaction.

Employers in manufacturing industry who have succeeded in controlling the accident hazards in their plants are familiar with this distinction. Pictures, posters, stunts, addresses, and any number of methods for securing immediate attention have been used, with no lasting effect on the accident record. Safe working conditions may be largely dependent on elimination of physical hazards. But safety is the result of a mental attitude. The channels for promoting safe working attitudes are channels which are constant rather than spectacular.

No permanent achievement in creating safe working habits has ever been possible on the basis of an intermittent attack. A startling poster showing the tragic result of indifference or thoughtlessness may catch the attention of every employee who passes the board where it is displayed. The impression will be made on the minds of most of them. But in most minds the impression will be either filed away as inactive material or actually forgotten, unless it can be in some way directly related to the daily task and environment. This connection between what happened somewhere else and what can happen here is almost never made by a quick glance at a picture or a slogan. And equally important is the recognition that one picture or one impression, no matter how vivid, will not create the permanent custom of safe thinking.

In the task of creating understanding, the result of spectacular stunts or announcements is likely to be positively bad instead of merely insufficient. If the item of information to be conveyed is spectacular or startling in itself, it surely does not need a spectacular announcement. If it is merely one of a hundred pieces of information to be shared with employees, the use of a startling form of announcement is likely to "high-light" the one item unduly, distort the true perspective, and create a barrier against securing proper attention to scores of other items to be made known later. Not all announcements can be startling. The attempt to maintain a high pitch of effort to attract attention, day after day and week after week, merely destroys all impressiveness of the separate communications.

The first element in the understanding which we should be trying to create is the understanding by employees that facts about the enterprise are not being concealed from them. The knowledge that they can get the information they want is more important than any actual information that can be given to them. Incidentally, in too many enterprises, this knowledge that he can get such information would be just about the most startling information which could be given to the average employee!

To promote this realization that information is frankly and honestly available, the method of conveying the information should be so casual that it cannot be distinguished from the normal conduct of the daily relationships. The media used should be so natural that they will fit perfectly into the structure of the organization with which the employee is already familiar.

Clearly this does not mean that no medium can be used

which has not already been identified as a part of the behavior pattern in the establishment. It does mean that no new medium can be first used in such a way as to direct attention to the medium instead of to the information. It does mean that no channel can be suddenly used which is contrary to the known character of the enterprise and its management.

To picture an extreme and imaginary case, we may assume a manufacturing corporation which for years has positively avoided any sharing of information with employees. It has followed a definite program of letting each workman know only what is necessary so that he may perform his assigned tasks. It has discouraged both workers and foremen from visiting other departments. It has avoided the adoption or publication of wage scales in the hope of concealing the wage rates of other workers. It has prohibited foremen from interesting themselves in the general subject of costs of production, to say nothing of costs of materials. It has guarded as state secrets the sources of its supplies, the marketing situation, the value of investment, the amount or rate of profits, and even the prospective operating schedule. If such a corporation were suddenly to announce that henceforth employees were welcome to information on some or any of these subjects, what might be the mental reaction of employees?

At first we might reasonably look for suspicion and skepticism. There might be a feeling that such a radical departure from past policy was insincere, or that it showed uneasiness about an approaching crisis and a desire to lead the employees into an attitude of sympathy with the bosses. It might imply, in the minds of employees, a confession of employer guilt or employer bad judgment in the past. The very substance of such an announcement must be the change of policy.

In other words, the corporation is saying in effect: "Up to now we have tried to keep you from knowing anything about the business. We have now decided that this was wrong.

We have now decided that you will do better work for us if you know more about the business. We have now decided that we can no longer keep this information away from you, since the government is going to publish it anyway. Therefore, we are going to turn over a new leaf and tell you anything you may ask, within reasonable limits, of course."

We may all agree that employee reaction to such an announcement is likely to be 90 per cent bad. But we may need to explore more carefully the reaction to an actual delivery of a certain amount of information, instead of a blanket announcement of a new policy. In this exploration, we may well conclude that the manner of conveying the information is the important question.

If the method used is noticeable, as compared with the past practices, the reaction is likely to be almost the same as to an announcement of conversion to a new policy. For such a corporation as we have pictured, the sudden appearance of Volume I, Number 1, of a house organ, carrying facts about the business which had hitherto been withheld, would incur the danger of the bad reaction we have surmised. So would the appearance of a bulletin board carrying a revelation of such facts, and so would the calling of an unprecedented mass meeting to hear the manager or president tell things which employees had never been supposed to know. So would a direct mail letter to each employee telling him how much profit the corporation was making.

But let us suppose the management of this imaginary corporation is sincere in its belief that the policy of the past has led to misunderstanding, sincere in the belief that the sharing of information with employees will help to create understanding, sincere in a determination to let the facts be known to those who are affected by the facts. What can this management do to put the new policy into effect without defeating its main purpose at the start? How can it avoid shocking employees and at the same time lead them to realize that they can know the facts about the enterprise which is a part of their lives?

There is no sudden way. There is no channel which can instantly make employees conscious of the new possibilities. Any pressing for sudden results, for sudden interest, greater confidence, and general acceptance of information by employees is hopeless. The first rule must be that the process of sharing information with employees is a gradual one. It follows that the building of employee confidence in the new policy is a slow and gradual task.

The second rule must be that this confidence must permeate the whole organization. It is useless, or worse, to hope that employees can be brought to this status of understanding unless every level of intermediate supervision has first accepted the policy. Therefore the process of sharing information must begin at the top levels of supervision and permeate the whole line and staff personnel. It is courting defeat to attempt to reach the wage earner with actual information, or with the consciousness that information is available, until his supervisor has first been reached.

A third rule is that the policy of sharing information with employees must be made effective through channels which are natural to the particular establishment. If there has existed a house organ of the strictly "gossip" type, ostensibly edited by employees, to tell personal news about employees, the columns of such a publication may be gradually used to reveal, as news, some of the business facts which have never been revealed before. If there has been a customary meeting of department heads or foremen to discuss immediate operating plans, or safety, or similar subjects, it provides a natural channel through which information on other subjects may begin to filter out.

These rather obvious rules have been drawn to fit an imaginary enterprise whose management has heretofore deliberately avoided sharing information with employees. They may not seem appropriate to an employer who has had no such deliberate policy but who has had no positive policy of sharing information with employees and no systematic plan for doing so. Are there any rules which we can consider proper for such an employer in selecting and using media for his program?

The three requirements of any plan already cited obtain here also. The media used for sharing information with employees must not be spectacular but must be customary. They must be of a type which will enable both the policy and the information to permeate the whole organization. They must be natural to the particular company or establishment.

A few other requirements of the program are generally acceptable, and have a direct bearing on the selection of media or implements. The program must be a continuous one, a method of conduct rather than a campaign. It must be an expanding one, permitting the delivery of ever more information as employees ask for it. It must be forever incidental to the actual conduct and management of the enterprise; that is, it must not become an institution apart from the actual work or operation of the enterprise, nor separated from the management, nor important in any way which overshadows the daily task of getting the work done.

In another volume, larger than this, someone else may write, or may have written already, a description of many methods and media which this volume does not even mention. In these chapters, there is no discussion of the use of films in general; on the various uses of this one medium a large book could be written, and several booklets have already been written. Films have been used in the coldly practical process of giving workers information about how to perform the manual processes of their jobs. They have been used to bring stimulating information to both industrial workers and sales clerks about the romance of the materials they handle. They have been used to follow the products of a factory or the services of a utility into the distant homes of ultimate consumers and put this information before employees. They have been used to acquaint employees in one unit with the personnel, activities, and surroundings of units located far away.

No discussion in this short book is directed to visits to other plants or visits to suppliers of materials or to distributors of products—visits by selected groups of employees, who return bringing their fresh and vital information in the form of reports to group meetings of their fellow workers. No special attention has been given to the sharing of information by means of group visits by employees to other departments in the same establishment.

We have not discussed the effective use of a plant or store library stocked with books and magazines dealing with the industry or business. Several chapters could be written about this method of sharing information—how to make the material available, how to encourage its use, where and when to recommend reading rooms and reading time.

We have omitted chapters which could be written about the sharing of information through news stories or paid space in local newspapers of general circulation. There is no mention of supply of display material for the use of public schools, interesting the worker at home through the curiosity of his boy or girl as stimulated in the classroom or school laboratory.

In the following pages we discuss only a few of the tools which may be used in such a program. We try to test them against the long-range purpose of the program. We try to test them against the standards described above. We try always to test them as to their proved or probable value in the fundamental effort to create understanding.

Fully recognizing the popularity of many of these methods, and the fact that tens of millions of dollars are being spent every year in their use, I confess a prejudice against any or all of them as a complete program. I recognize immense value in some of them, an undeniable need for most of them. But I frankly approach the discussion in the belief that no one of them, nor all of them combined, will meet the requirements set up in this chapter.

The proposition to which I hope to lead is that the best of them, selected to fit the exact conditions of a single company, will do the most that they can do when they have invited the flow of information through the natural, functional line organization, the supervisory personnel of that company.

X

GETTING THE EMPLOYEE TO TUNE IN

During most of the hours of the day the air is full of music, soap operas, market news, war news, sport news, cooking recipes, political speeches, educational lectures, police calls. Hundreds of programs are being broadcast at once, at least a dozen within range of your own receiving set. But unless you turn on your radio and tune it to one of the broadcasting stations, you hear no program. If you turn it on and tune it to one station, you hear none of the other programs.

The industrial world is full of information for employees. Some of it is correct and complete. Some of it is correct but incomplete. Much of it is mixed with misinterpretations, favorable or unfavorable. Some of it is positive misinformation.

It is broadcast, or "released," or spread, in many ways. It goes out over the air. It is "planted" in newspaper stories. It is press-agented into magazine articles. It appears in official reports of corporations, trade organizations, labor unions, and government agencies. It is posted on bulletin boards, printed on payroll inserts, typed in direct-mail letters, carried on the grapevine. It is "spouted" by propagandists for big business, little business, the free-enterprise system, and the overburdened taxpayer. It is preached by propagandists for organized labor, the unemployed, the senior citizens, the underprivileged.

Very little of it is actually received by the prospective listeners for whom it is intended. The human mind can be "tuned in" on only one source of information at any one time. When one's mind is so "tuned in," all other efforts to "inform" him are ineffective. When he has not "tuned in" on any source of information, when he is not mentally listening, all the facts and propaganda pass him by.

We are "tuned in" most of the time, we are mentally listening to something. And when we are listening to something, we are excluding almost everything else. When we are listening to our own re-broadcast of Sunday's catch of fish, we are not hearing Joe's red-hot tip about the new trucks the boss is buying. When we are "tuned in" on the memory of the last words from the wife this morning about Jimmie's eye trouble, we are not mentally receiving the news on the payroll stuffer about the increase in the company's taxes.

The employer who has modernized his thinking to the degree of wanting his employees to share information about the business has gone a long way forward. But he still has a long road ahead. He cannot even begin to share that information with his employees until his employees want it. Employees and all the rest of us are masters, each of his own mental receiving set. No amount of facts will register in our minds if to us they are "facts not worth knowing." The president of the company may address a letter to every employee, telling him the truth about the radical increase in raw material costs or the loss of export markets. The message will not "carry" to the employee whose mental receiver is tuned for an explanation of the big salary which gossip says that same president receives.

The average employer who wants to share information with his employees demonstrates in himself this principle of "tuning in." His mind is possessed by the idea that his employees should know about taxes or depreciation or the current slump in sales. "Tuned in" mentally to the thought of sharing with his employees the particular information he wants them to have, he refuses to "tune in" on the questions they are asking.

If the commercial radio receiving sets are built for frequencies of 560 to 1650 kilocycles (56 to 165 on your dial), no broadcaster will be wise in securing a wave length outside this standard band. He would reject with irritation the sales argument that a short-wave transmitter will reach Japan, that a long-wave transmitter will reach the Stratoliner flying over Texas. *He knows* that the radio sets he wants to reach are built for standard wave-length bands. If he can secure a wave length within that band, at least the sets *can* be tuned in on his broadcasts. As employers, we have frequently launched into campaigns of sharing information with employees without even exploring the question of the wave-length band within which they can receive information.

This ability to receive is not a result or expression of mental capacity or intelligence. It is a result of daily life interests. For the overwhelming majority of us, our ability to receive information effectively is determined by the span of our daily life interests.

If I am a wheat grower or a manufacturer of wooden mouse traps, it is almost sure that I will not "receive" the story you are telling me about the nonoxidizing properties of a new metal-plating process. And yet I may be just as intelligent as you. If you are a wholesale hardware merchant, faced with a shortage of galvanized nails, it is almost certain that you will not "receive" the very important information I am trying to give you about the discovery that the waste material from my meat-packing plant can now be sold as a base for road paving. But that is no reflection on your mental capacity. When our employees want to know whether the plant will run full after Christmas, it is almost certain that they will not "receive" our bulletin-board "propaganda" about the burden of our social security taxes for the year.

Assuming our willingness, as employers, to share information with employees, the next step is to realize that the only information we *can* share with them is information which they want. We must patiently, wisely, and correctly learn what information they do want. That does not mean that the information they want today is all they will ever want; that it is all the information we can ever share with them. Nor does it mean that there is no part for us to play in helping them to enlarge their desire for information.

When an employee, for reasons which are rooted in the experiences of his daily life, wants to know about the unemployment compensation he will receive during next month's shutdown, we should be ready to give him that information. We should be ready, because having and giving that information is one of the services we must trade for the kind of service and attitude we want from him.

But we must be ready also for another reason. When he asks about his own personal benefit under this particular law, and when we give him the information on that, the occasion is perfect to remind him where the money comes from to pay these benefits. Such facts as the required "waiting period" are logical leaders to facts about the relative amount of unemployment in our industry and others. The method of registration gives the opportunity to explain the amount of local unemployment as shown by registrations at the local Employment Service office and our effort to co-operate with the Employment Service. All or any of these details which he wants are logical vehicles on which to carry to his mind the fact that our unemployment and other social security taxes are costing us so much per year. That in turn may enable us to inform him, and have him "receive" the information, that our social security tax is equal to twice our whole cost of fire insurance.

This process of using a ready-made interest in a subject as the means of creating an interest in a related subject is the foundation of successful radio "education." The reader can recognize it in any one of a dozen programs with which he is familiar. If we find out and list the information employees *want,* and the information we want to share with them, we are sure to see some overlapping in the two lists. The areas of overlapping are the fields in which we must begin the sharing of information with employees. They are the wave lengths within which employees will "receive" and within which we must "release" our information to them.

But besides bringing our information within the bounds of the subject matter in which the employee is initially interested, we must also make it available at a time when he is inclined to "tune in." A period of depressed or declining business is no time to begin sharing information with employees. If we have not begun the practice earlier we must be wise enough to wait for another, better time. The impulse to solicit the sympathetic understanding of employees in a period of stress is one which we all tend to obey. In fact, such times produce many conversions to the faith and practice of taking our employees into our confidence. But no deep knowledge of psychology is needed to tell us that a program of information for employees adopted and launched at such a time has little chance to do its work.

We can, on this question, use our own reactions to measure those of the other man. These reactions are so basic, so natural, that here we can think as we would think if we were employees. After years of silence, secretiveness, concealment of "confidential" facts, and grudging release of information under pressure, an employer who approached us with a sudden change of front would arouse our suspicion rather than our interest. If during the days of good business he had considered us incapable of understanding the facts of business life, he could hardly expect us to listen to hard-luck stories when they prevail.

Many of these conversions last only through the days of the employer's acute need for sympathy and co-operation from his employees. Many of them are conversions to the expediency of telling employees the nature of the trouble during bad times, so that they will understand, work harder, be patient on questions of wages, be alert to curtailing wastes of time and materials. Few of them are conversions to the basic faith in the everlasting precept that "knowledge bringeth understanding."

Perhaps employees are not better able to understand the information we may share with them, in bad times, than in good times. Perhaps it is we who have a clearer understanding, in bad times, that some of the things we want from employees cannot be had unless they know some things we have not let them know.

If our willingness to share information with employees is frankly temporary, if it is merely a willingness to pay that particular price for co-operation during a period of stress, we may as well save ourselves the effort. Any facts, any information, offered as the basis of a plan for sympathetic understanding then will be wasted as would be the advertising broadcast while the people within the range of the station are normally asleep. The short-term policy of sharing information with employees will not buy even the short-term result of understanding co-operation.

But it is reasonable to expect that the experience of a depression period will bring many employers to a lasting realization of the need of sharing information with employees. Discouraging attitudes, brought to view under the spotlight of the difficult days, can be traced to a lack of understanding. The lack of understanding can be traced to our long-time failure to share with employees the information which is a part of our mutual industrial or business relationship.

To an employee, curtailed employment, loss of customary overtime work, plant shutdowns, all these incidents of depressed business, are hard facts. They are facts that hurt. They force postponement of the new rug or the new car, of Johnnie's college or Janie's music lessons, of the new dress for the wife or the tonsil operation for the boy. Because they hurt, because the hurt is real, and because the cause is invisible, resentment smolders. The smoldering resentment seeks a victim. In the absence of knowledge with which to reason things through, the resentment is likely to strike at the immediate channel through which the hurt has come.

Somewhere in the employer group is the one who seems to have decreed the shutdown, the wage cut, or the layoff. At least, there is the man who broke the news—and expression of the resentment comes in surly unfriendliness to the foreman or the timekeeper, slowing down to make what work there is last longer, and loose talk about the oppression of the worker and the selfishness of the employer and the employer class.

It is useless to complain of the unfairness of these reactions. This thinking and feeling would be our thinking and feeling under the sting of the same hurt and under the same cloud of lack of information.

So, faced with the bitter realization that a hundred or a thousand men who work with us, think and feel and act in ways that make the difficulties greater for us and for them, we may easily awaken to the everlasting need for the knowledge that "bringeth understanding." And in the brightness of this awakening we may decide to launch out immediately on a campaign of sharing information with our employees.

But the time is not right for getting the employee to "tune in." If we begin with facts to show that causes beyond our control have caused the recession of business and curtailment of earnings, we get a hearing, it is true—but a hearing which consumes our facts in the fires of skepticism, suspicion, and disbelief, fires which flame out of the smoldering resentment.

Starting on the defensive is the wrong way to start sharing information with employees. Of course, we could begin sharing other information which is basic and not defensive. If we reach our decision on the policy during a period of poor business, no profits, low employment, and low earnings, we need not start sharing only that information which seems designed to prove that we are not to blame for the slump. We can begin with information which has none of the aspects of an alibi. But the mind of the employee is already "tuned in" on a competing program which hampers our efforts.

The mind of the average American is a naturally sensitive receiving instrument. Through the years of the growth of mass employment, the instrument has not been invited to "tune in" on basic information from which understanding of the free-enterprise system can grow. It has not been invited to "tune in" on facts about industry and business, particularly about the business in which it is engaged. The broadcasts of wrongly directed resentment can be readily received during days of depression. Failure to share with employees the information which would lead to understanding has left them ready to "tune in" on the suggestions which create misunderstanding.

When these ideas have started to grow, we are unwise to start broadcasting our valuable information. We have before us a patient job of preparing the receiving attitude, the willingness to "tune in" on our program. Before we broadcast to employees the facts we want them to know, the facts we think they need to know, we must be realistic enough to find out what facts they want to know. But we must also be realistic to see whether or not now is the appropriate time.

If an employer during a business slump sees the need of sharing information with employees, so that he may get their understanding, it would seem that we should rejoice and urge him to go ahead, to obey that impulse, before he changes his mind. But, although we may rejoice, we must urge him to bide his time, for these reasons:

1. While they are worried about curtailed and unstable earnings, employees are not willing to "tune in" on messages about anything else.
2. If he gives them facts, at such a time, about the causes of the depression, such facts will be met with suspicion and disbelief and regarded as efforts to create an alibi.
3. The practice of sharing information with employees must

build slowly, starting at a time when it is neither a defense against criticism nor the obvious grinding of an ax.

4. Preparation, confidence, attention are essential to a program of sharing information with employees. They are inconsistent with starting the program under pressure.

In contrast to a period of depression, there are features of public attitude which make this year of 1942 an almost perfect occasion for entering upon, or expanding, a program of sharing information with employees. The range of subject matter on which the mind of each of us is ready to "tune in" has been greatly increased. The defense program has widened the mental interests of tens of millions of us.

At no time within the span of our generation has such unity of thinking and purpose possessed the minds of men and women in every walk of American life. The period of utmost American effort in 1918–1919 brought no such unity. The reaction then was partly idealistic, partly nationalistic, largely emotional. It did not approach the conscious, reasoning discrimination of today, when the overwhelming majority of us have comprehended the basic conflict—the concept of sacred personality and individual freedom desperately threatened by the totalitarian concept.

Minds which a year ago would "tune in" only on subjects such as wages, rents, movies, baseball, and more wages are ready today for a whole new range of information. Military and industrial needs for men, chances for new jobs, increased living costs, taxes reaching lower incomes than ever, strikes in defense industries, curtailment of whole enterprises because of priorities—these and a hundred new topics have caught these minds. It is a day when enlightened employers can share information with employees more acceptably than ever before. The employee will "tune in" today. *If he acquires the information, there is hope of creating the understanding which will save the American enterprise system in the days of confusion and reaction which will surely follow.*

XI

THE BULLETIN BOARD

One of the first means of conveying information to employees which naturally suggests itself is the bulletin board. Conveying information seems to be the prime purpose of any bulletin board. In some form, the bulletin board is found in almost every place where people congregate. We see it in the railroad, bus, or airport waiting rooms. Usually we find two forms of it in such places. One form conveys specific information which is likely to be desired by the people who come to the waiting room, in other words, timetable facts about arrivals and departures and about delays. The other carries advertising—displays notices or descriptions of services which the observer may be induced to buy. He may have come to meet a friend and, while waiting, be attracted by a picture of the seashore or mountain resort, accompanied by information on how easily and cheaply the paradise can be reached over "our lines."

We see the bulletin board in front of churches, usually giving specific information which is likely to be desired by the observer who deliberately stops to read. What kind of a church is this? Who is the minister? At what times are the services held? But we also see an occasional attempt to use the bulletin board outside the church for appeal purposes. Sometimes it carries a striking name, line, or picture calculated to attract the attention of the casual observer. It may be the name of some national figure with the promise that he "will speak here Sunday." It may be a spectacular promise of a free musical program. It may be a picture related to some currently discussed news—the abdicated king, the deceased Senator, the ruins of a bombed or burned cathedral.

In some way, the attention which has been caught by the words or the picture will be directed toward interest in the services or program of the church. Sometimes the bulletin outside the church attempts to convey the essence of a sermon in ten words or less; perhaps even here the real hope is to attract the attention of the casual reader.

The billboard for poster advertising is an adaptation of the bulletin board. It tries to attract the attention of the reader, to create an interest in an article, a service, or a program, and to suggest to him what to do about it. In some public places, such as courthouses and jails, we see bulletin boards at work again. They carry pictures and descriptions of wanted criminals and offers of rewards for their capture—another appeal to our attention, interest, and co-operative action. The warning that taxes are due day after tomorrow has the same general purpose; the difference is that it seems to threaten us instead of to offer to reward us.

We are within sight of bulletin boards of one kind or another for a surprisingly large portion of our waking hours, so much so that we accept them as natural factors in our lives without even recognizing them as bulletin boards. But in the course of a few minutes' thought most of us will discover that we agree on several reactions to bulletin boards, billboards, and posters in general.

We subconsciously appreciate bulletin boards which do us a service. We are glad to be told, through this medium, the things we want to know. If we are interested in going to church or going for a trip, we like to find the desired information given clearly, briefly, and at the place where we are likely to look for it.

We subconsciously resent bulletin boards which intrude on us at inappropriate places. Most of us react unfavorably to the high-powered picture of a finger pointing rudely at our noses, with the legend "YOU should drive the new Rattler 8!" We do not appreciate even desired information offered on a crowded bulletin board, or in a form which is difficult to grasp. We all feel vaguely dissatisfied with a board which carries a long textual message, so long that we cannot read it all in the time we naturally spend in that waiting room or at that highway intersection.

Assuming the conditions of a typical business establishment—manufacturing, mercantile, or other—what can be said of the bulletin board as a means for carrying information to employees?

Every employee can see it. Compared with any other medium, it has positive "circulation." If there is one entrance used by all employees, one board can be placed there. If several entrances are used, one board can be placed at each.

But no employee is likely to see such a bulletin board for very long at a time. Rules and customs discourage loitering at entrances and exits. All employees on a shift come to work at the same time and leave at the same time. The entrance, exit, or "clock alley" is not a practical place to stand while one reads a lengthy bulletin.

Every employee can see a bulletin board and probably he can give the notice a more careful reading if it is placed in the department where he works. But even there the time for reading a long notice may be lacking. Generally the only time available will be company time. It must be an important message which will induce the average employer or foreman to encourage men to pause in their work for several minutes of reading time. But even if it is rated as that important by the employer, it may not be so rated by the employee.

Another favored place for the bulletin board is an employees' lunch room, or a smoking room, if one exists. In such a place there is less pressure for time. There is more feeling of ease and relaxation. Time the employee spends there usually is not company time. Surely, some of us say, we should try to get employees to use their own time to read the bulletins we post for them.

But there is another view about this kind of time. It belongs to the employee, and he is usually quite conscious of this fact. He is usually inclined to assert his ownership of the time. If he is in the lunch room, he is there to eat, and the lunch hour is a part of his day which he has not leased to the employer. If there is more time than he needs for eating, he may want to use it for rest, for conversation, for a quick game of some kind. Without wording his thoughts, he is likely to have the same vague resentment we all have to a bulletin or poster which seems to intrude. He may think we have a lot of nerve, expecting him to use his own lunch hour to read our blasted propaganda!

Wherever placed, a bulletin board offers the chance to use dramatic, colorful material: news pictures, cartoons, spectacular charts can be displayed. To a certain extent, the bulletin board so used becomes a billboard.

Even as common and usable a medium as the bulletin board is affected by the same need as any other medium, the need for catching attention. By considering the effectiveness of "eye-catchers," we admit that the bulletin board has no automatic entry to the mind of the employee. We admit that he may pass it by unless something on it flashes across to his observation. The task of finding an attention-catching display which leads logically to the message to be conveyed is a difficult one. It has been well done in safety posters, not so well in any other subject field.

The bulletin board is sometimes described in terms which mean that it is dignified, that it is conservative, that it is democratic. But it is essentially a tool of management, the property of the employer, the voice of the company. Its use is controlled by management and can be confined to material which has the approval of management.

It reaches all observers with a suggestion of equal respect. The same message, in the same words, through the same medium, is offered to the errand boy, the janitor, and the chief mechanic. But to one standing in front of the bulletin board as a worker, instead of behind it as an employer, the same admitted facts may produce quite a different reaction. It is a tool of management. Therefore nothing is going to be on it except "what the brass hats want to put across to us. Of course, we can all get the same dope off the bulletin board, but what do I care about that propaganda stuff? Why should I bother to read it just because the big guy wants to get it across to all of us? It may be swallowed by some of these fellows, but I'm not falling for any stuff that doesn't put dollars in my pay check!"

Both logic and careful observation lead to similar conclusions about the bulletin board as a medium for sharing information with employees. It seems to be the most effective if not the only effective medium for certain kinds of information. For other types of information it seems to be less effective, sometimes ineffective, and often objectionable because of reactions to the method rather than the subject matter.

The degrees of effectiveness, and of favorable or unfavorable reaction, are identical with those found in the use of bulletin boards in general. In general we appreciate brief, accurate, well-placed bulletins, conveying information which we want, at the time and in the place we want it. In the same way employees seem to appreciate the bulletin board when its use meets these standards. We resent bulletins which are inappropriately placed, offensive or intrusive in style, inconveniently long, or too persuasive in tone. So do employees in general.

Information which should reach all employees, because it tells something they want to know, belongs on a bulletin board. If the establishment is to be closed next Monday, a notice to that effect is a logical item for the bulletin board; similarly, if daylight-saving hours are to be observed beginning next week or if there is to be a general shutdown for repairs or inventory. If employees are invited to record their desires as to selection of vacation dates, the bulletin board offers a good medium to announce that fact. If a general change in wage rates is about to go into effect, as a result either of collective bargaining or of other causes, such as the Fair Labor Standards Act, the bulletin board can well carry the news.

If a new manager, superintendent, or other supervisor has been named, and if his responsibility extends to the whole establishment, the general bulletin board is a fairly good medium through which to say so. If it is a new supervisor whose functions are confined to a department, and there is a bulletin board in that department, it is a courteous and effective thing to make the announcement on that board. In either case, the bulletin board is by no means the best medium.

When an important executive of the company has passed away, the bulletin board is an excellent and natural place in which to convey that information to all employees. When some law or governmental regulation has been adopted which obviously affects the activities of the entire business, employees will receive the information through the bulletin board with appreciation. For instance, it would be well to announce briefly on the bulletin board that a defense order places the principal raw material on the priority list for defense production and that nondefense uses will be curtailed. When aliens are required to register, notice to that effect belongs on the bulletin board.

If the local schools are offering courses in related work for such employees as maintenance mechanics or operators of certain machines, a bulletin board which will be seen by those who may be interested can effectively carry the announcement. If the annual report of the corporation is offered to employees upon request, the offer may be posted on the bulletin board—although other methods are usually more effective for such announcement.

Some institutions have actually made a bulletin out of

the entire annual report, all pages exposed for easy reading, and posted it on the board. If the management has hopes that any considerable number of employees will thus read the report—well, that is optimism.

If the president of the company has written or read an article on the economics of the industry, or the relative wages in this and other competitive areas, an article which he thinks is good, he may be tempted to put it on the bulletin board. Probably he should think again and resist the temptation.

A current magazine article may tell some interesting facts about the industry or business or about the particular establishment, or about one of its personalities, and thus generate pride or satisfaction in anyone connected with the institution. Should the bulletin board be used as a place to display the article for all to see and read? Hardly; but the article may be effectively announced there. Perhaps the title can be cut out and posted, with advice as to how to obtain the article. A picture of the home-town boy who appears in the article may attract attention; two or three lines may tell where to see the article.

Examples of effective and ineffective uses of the bulletin board can be multiplied indefinitely. It is more profitable to try to find a pattern into which they will fit. A few simple rules seem to emerge as the general dimensions of this pattern. Because they are generalizations, they are subject to modification in different places, cases, and times. But as generalizations, they will help toward using the bulletin board as a positive factor in sharing information.

1. Any message on a bulletin board must be brief. Arbitrarily, it should aim at a maximum reading time of thirty seconds.
2. All such messages must be current; they must be "flash" messages related to immediate events or immediate future actions.
3. Any such message should tell something the employee

wants to know—about working schedules, wages, rules, and privileges.

4. These messages should be confined to those which assist the employee in guiding his positive actions, such as coming to work, planning a vacation or registering for the draft.
5. When lengthy information, or information which only indirectly interests the employee, is to be offered to him, the item can meet the standards of good bulletin-board usage; the information as a whole (the annual report, for example) cannot. The item in this case can be brief, and can tell how and where the complete article or report can be seen.

One final rule which is broader than the others needs to be observed. There is certain work which the bulletin board *must* perform. We depend on it as one important link in the chain to carry specific instructions about working schedules and activities, instructions which must reach all employees, which must be understood, and which usually must be acted upon. If we clutter up the bulletin board with extraneous matter, lengthy articles, propaganda, educational information, we destroy the character of this medium as a place for information which is of "flash" importance. Too much material of any kind will lead to a growing disregard of the bulletin board. Then we can no longer depend on it as a medium for telling and emphasizing those things which are important to our immediate operating plans.

XII

THE PAY INSERT

The employees with whom we think of sharing information work for wages. A universal feature of our relationship with them is that of paying them their earned wages at short intervals. It is one of the facts of our common life, whether the wages are paid in money placed in an envelope or counted from our hands into theirs, or in the form of checks bearing their names as payees and our names as makers or signers; whether the wages are computed on the passage of calendar periods at so much per week or per month, on the basis of hours worked or that of measured production or on any combination of these bases.

Since the delivery or payment of wages earned is universal in our relations with employees, the occasion appeals to many employers as a natural and ideal one for delivering "educational" messages to employees. The delivery has unique advantages: It reaches every employee, more surely than any other medium. It occurs at a time of automatic attention; the employee is alert to the arrival of his check or envelope, ready to look at it to check its correctness in some cases, perhaps even to see if it reflects a raise. Moreover, he cannot refuse to take it. And almost always in the case of family men the envelope or the check will go home and be seen by the wife.

A message so delivered is not subject to the same requirement of brevity which applies to an item on the bulletin board. Because it is going home with the employee, it can be read at his leisure. We can make it as long or as short as we wish.

The form is easy to use for the delivery of messages. If a check is used, the message may be loosely attached, either on a slip no larger than the check or on a larger sheet in which the check may be folded. Or an envelope with the message on the outside may be used to enclose the check; he must open the envelope to get the check. If payment is made in cash in the customary "pay envelope," again the message may be on the outside, close to the notice of the amount or calculation. Or the message may be on what is, with strict accuracy, referred to as an "insert," a slip inserted into the envelope with the money.

The advantages cited above are largely in terms of time, uniformity, and mechanical simplicity. They cannot be seriously discounted. But, like all other media for sharing information, this one of pay inserts must also be appraised or valued by other measurements.

To give facts or information in printed or written form, to get facts or information into the hands of employees, is not what we mean by sharing information with them. To get information into the hands of an employee does not promise the real objective of getting it into his mind and thought. One other measurement of value which we must apply to every medium for conveying information is that of its effectiveness in carrying through to his mind, to his thinking processes. Although the word seems vague and academic, we have no better name for this standard than "psychological."

A high recommendation for the medium of pay inserts, in terms of time, uniformity, and simplicity, does not guarantee that this medium will also be entitled to recommendation when appraised for its psychological effectiveness. In studying this or any other medium, we may even find that the advantages on the practical scale actually create disadvantages on the psychological scale.

We have noted that the pay check or pay envelope reaches every employee. This may not suggest any psychological disadvantage, but certainly it is not a guaranty of value in terms of psychological effectiveness. It requires the identical form of presentation to all, which is rarely effective in complete measure. Even if the same information needs to be carried to all employees, the same form may not carry it to all; it may carry it to the hands of all, but not necessarily to the minds of all. The very knowledge that the same message is being delivered, in the same form, to every other person on the payroll may result in creating a resistance, in your mind or mine, to the acceptance of the message. We may receive it with our hands or even our eyes and still refuse to tune in our minds on it because we resent being treated as one of the herd rather than as a person. The message or document thus delivered may be depreciated merely because it is indiscriminately distributed.

It is true that such a message may be personalized. It may speak to me as "My friend"; but I am likely to react as you do when some radio voice says, "My friends": you think immediately of the millions of other listeners hearing the same greeting and to some extent you stand aside and listen to the message as being delivered to them rather than as a message intended for you. The pay-envelope message may bear the signature of the president of the company, but the fact that every other employee receives the same message with the same signature offsets that.

True, also, the pay insert reaches the employee at a time of automatic attention; in the language of chapter x he is already "tuned in." But on just what is he tuned in? Let us follow the steps of development of this attention, the twirling of the dial of his mental radio:

First. It is payday. I should get my pay today [the radio is switched on].

Second. There should be $9.60 extra for that eight hours last Saturday at time-and-one-half. Maybe they will take out for that tool I lost. I suppose that collector will be around again tomorrow for the furniture payment. It's about time I was getting another raise. [The radio is accurately tuned to his personal concern about his personal pay—whether it is figured correctly, what he must do with it this payday, how it may be improved.]

With this tuning, with this automatic attention, is it a good time for us to insert a "commercial," to expect to attract the mind of Mr. Employee to the increase of customers' complaints on quality, or to the size of the company's tax bill? If not, it is worse than idle to give him a message about these things along with the pay check or envelope on which his attention is centered. It is not comparable merely to the injection of a "commerical" for Kasey's Kidney Kapsules at the pause in the broadcast of the World's Series Game; it is more like the addition of a second broadcaster at a second microphone when there is no pause in the Series broadcast.

The comment has been made that the employee cannot refuse to take his pay check or pay envelope and the slip bearing our message can be so attached or integrated that he cannot refuse to take it either. Unquestionably, we have him in a position where he cannot avoid taking our message into his hands. But between his hands or his eyes and the mysterious thing called his mind there is a wide gulf. He must take our printed words into his hands. It is likely but not sure that he will read them with his eyes. But even then he is master of his mind and need not accept our message. The very fact that we have forced it into his hands when he cannot refuse to take it raises the probability that his human reaction will be to refuse to accept it into his mind.

Another physical advantage of pay inserts is that in most cases they will also reach the wife of the married employee. This advantage is duplicated in the appraisal of psychological values. The occasional resentment of an employee because we have given him a message which he cannot avoid showing to "the wife" is not serious. This feature in itself is wholly good.

There is a final consideration which may outweigh all

others. When payday arrives the employee has already done everything he is obliged to do, to earn the wages due. He has performed his part of the bargain, and performed it in advance. He has not agreed to go farther and read our "propaganda" before he gets possession of the wages we owe him. He already has a clear title to the money in that envelope or represented by that check.

If we can separate the features of ethics and good taste from the other features of our relations with employees, it is bad ethics and bad taste to require him, in effect, to do something else for us before he can get possession of the money he has already earned. His implied contract is that he will render certain service for which he is entitled to certain pay. There is no implication that, having rendered this service, he must also accept a piece of information which we want him to have but for which he has not asked.

Ignoring the standard of ethics and good taste, but conceding the facts and reasoning set forth above, it is simply not good business to expect favorable reception of educational messages given to employees in this way.

A definite and emphatic difference should be recognized when the pay insert carries a message to which the employee is already tuned in, a message which is actually related to his particular pay check or pay envelope. In most cases this will not be a uniform, printed, or stereotyped message to all employees. It may be a personal message to John Smith, that his rate has been raised, that part of his earnings have been garnisheed, that his debt to the Credit Union has been paid and no further deduction is being made, that the extra check or amount included is the vacation pay to which he is entitled either under the company plan or under the union agreement.

But there are types of messages that may be uniform and printed or stereotyped, to all employees, which can well and wisely be "inserted" with the pay or pay check. In a number of carefully observed cases, no traces of poor reaction to this method of conveying information of these types has been evident.

One of these is a message announcing a general pay increase. If the increase is uniform, in cents per hour, dollars per week, or percentage, for all employees involved, there is no possible objection to a uniform announcement or explanation in the form of a payroll insert, either with the last wage payment at the old rate or with the first payment at the new rate. Of course, the amount of the increase may not be satisfactory; if it were a reduction, it surely would bring no satisfaction. But there is no likelihood of resentment against this method of announcement, because the message is intimately related to the pay check or wage money.

Similarly, if it has been decided to pay by check instead of in cash, or the reverse, that is a good subject for a pay insert. In fact, it is a subject which calls for full explanation, in this or some other way, in order to avoid needless misunderstandings such as have sometimes followed an entirely proper change in method of pay without the courtesy of advance explanation.

Another type of justifiable "pay insert" is the message from some managements offering some such document as the annual report of the corporation if the employee will but ask for a copy. A brief courteous statement that the report is available, with no pressure or "sales talk," and a convenient request card for the employee's use, are likely to produce a friendly reaction. While the message is not related to the pay, it has no flavor of intrusion. The employer is not asking the employee to do something, believe something, or even say something. He is free to throw away the announcement and the request card if he is not interested. The entire offer can be clearly one which he can accept if he wishes, not one which the employer wants him to accept.

As suggested in the chapter on the annual report, this offer to supply the report on request is preferable to an indiscriminate delivery of the report to employees. It is preferable, for results, to a similar announcement on the bulletin board. It is probably less effective than a direct-mail offer, as will be suggested later.

The annual report has been selected as a common example of the type of material which can be offered, with reasonable justification, by means of a pay insert. Other examples will occur to the reader, such as a newly published history of the company or of its home town or an interesting souvenir publication.

The types of uniform message which can wisely be put in the form of a pay insert are rare indeed. Use of the pay insert should ordinarily be infrequent. An exception can be admitted in the case of an employer who, through a long period, has established a tradition of supplying information to his employees in this way. To break that tradition, for the reason that this is not theoretically a good way to supply information to employees, would be unwise, if the inserts have been accepted by employees as a matter of habit.

Any message may properly be carried in a pay insert if it basically relates to the pay check or pay envelope. If it is part and parcel of the make-up of the pay, it is a message on which the employee's mind is already tuned in. But it is incorrect, ethically, psychologically, and therefore practically, to use the pay insert to tell employees that we have acquired a new source of raw material, that we are facing new import competition, or that the president of the company didn't really get the $150,000 reported in the papers but had to give up $98,958 of it for federal income and defense taxes. Both ethically and practically, it is the wrong time and method for any message of the kind we class as educational, or inspiring, or morale-building—the wrong time and method for any message the employee or his critical friend can call propaganda.

The pay check or pay envelope belongs to the employee, with no strings attached. He feels that way about it. If we have a message which is a natural part of the transaction of giving him his pay, let us give it to him with the pay. If we have an educational message, unrelated to his pay, let us try to give it to him under conditions which logically promise a more willing and concentrated attention.

XIII

THE ANNUAL REPORT

Several influences have operated to change the form and use of annual reports of corporations. We have mentioned the volume of legislation and regulation which has forced the disclosure of facts once considered confidential. Without doubt these requirements have led to the making of annual reports which are more complete, more frank, and more understandable.

A second influence has been the drive against holding companies. A pure holding company with ten direct subsidiaries and forty subsidiaries of subsidiaries had very little to say to its own stockholders. Likewise for each of the subsidiary corporations on any level, there was no need for a published annual report to stockholders—the real stockholder, the parent corporation, already had full access to the books, often actually did the bookkeeping.

If there were public holdings of stock, in one or more of the subsidiaries, in addition to the controlling stock belonging to the parent holding company, it was common practice to give these "outsiders" the minimum of information. Why complicate their lives with questions about inter-company sales, management fees, duplicate salaries, and such practices of the typical pyramid in the 1920's?

The consolidated report of the parent company and all its subsidiaries could not attempt to picture the activities of each operating company—the first, second, and third degrees of inter-ownership; the allocation of the many varieties of funded debt, and the interchange of services or service charges. There might be seventeen bond issues secured by mortgages; one mortgage covering land owned by Company B, another covering equipment owned by Company C and leased to Company D for a fixed rental, and so on. There might be another bond issue secured by a trust indenture covering the revenues of Company E which were derived solely from royalties collected from Company F, and another debenture bond issue of Company G secured by a pledge of 70 per cent of the common stock of Company H and 55 per cent of the common stock of Company I, both owned by Company G. It was not surprising that the annual report of the parent company could say, as to funded debt, little more than this:

> Consolidated Bonded Debt of Company A and all Subsidiaries (detailed schedule available on request from First-Second Trust Company, New York) $40,000,000.00

The same practical difficulty existed in any attempt to reflect gross and net income, expenses, and ratio of current assets to current liabilities. The result in too many cases was consolidated confusion.

The drive against holding companies has changed this picture. Hundreds of corporate structures have been simplified by consolidations and mergers, by sales of subsidiaries, or by direct distribution of the stock of subsidiaries to the stockholders of the parent company. The actual facts to be reported today are such that they can be reported intelligently. The actual stockholders today are persons, interested in those facts. As a consequence, more annual reports are issued, and they tell more facts.

Added to compulsory reporting in some cases and elimination of holding companies in others has been the enlightened desire of corporation management to get closer to its stockholders, to manage their investments wisely and report on their management, and to awaken the interest of stockholders in some of the problems of management such as oppressive taxes or government regulation.

Another expression of this enlightenment has been the

desire to get closer to employees. Recent years have witnessed an astonishing growth in the practice of reporting to employees as well as to stockholders. The growth has been from almost none to scores of corporations which report to employees. But the "scores" are probably less than 10 per cent of the larger corporations of the country.

However, the annual report of a corporation has become suddenly an important medium for sharing information with employees, even if its importance is measured only by the number of employees who now receive reports. It is of the greatest possible importance when measured by its potential future influence on the free-enterprise system. This potential influence should be pictured, at least briefly, before we approach the technique of sharing information with employees through this medium.

The effect or influence on so-called top management is not the least important of the results. The debates over giving the annual report to employees, for the first time, have enabled many a conservative director and executive to take stock of his own attitude in a new way.

One actual conversation illustrates the mild shock of this inventory. In one large corporation, a junior executive was urging that the annual report go to employees. A typically conservative elder statesman announced with finality:

"The whole idea is wrong. The employees are certainly not entitled to any information the stockholders do not have."

"I agree with you," said the younger man. "But I'm not asking to give them anything the stockholders do not get."

"Well, how much could the average employee understand of our last report to stockholders?" said the senior. "How much sense could he make out of it?"

"Not much," admitted the younger man. "But how about the average stockholder?"

As a result, the annual report of that corporation underwent a transformation. It became a document designed to tell a story to anyone who can read, not merely to bankers and accountants as before. It became an attractive piece of printing, alive, colorful, simple, and expressive. And the officers of that corporation are firm in the belief that the facts of the life of the business belong to those in whose interest the officers manage. They have gone further, to the belief that employees have a stake, a right, and an interest in that information, an interest different in origin from but just as definite as that of the stockholders.

The decision to offer the annual report to the employees, and the evolution of the report so that it may be understandable, have changed the attitude of executives toward the whole subject of their relations with employees. It is not an exaggeration to say that this decision has in some cases influenced the policies of management throughout the business year. With adequate reporting to employees, and to stockholders as well, there is a constant incentive to avoid acts of management which would make embarrassing reading.

The technique of getting the annual report to employees is a matter of debate. There are wide differences of opinion, and of practice.

Should the same report go to stockholders and to employees? Students and observers disagree. Some of the best writing on the subject includes positive advice against using the same report. One writer points out that the report to employees needs to be simple, nontechnical, illustrated if possible, and attractive in appearance, while the report to stockholders probably needs to be dignified and so forth.

All such conclusions, and their supporting arguments, are subject to challenge. For instance, is there any reason to believe that the report to stockholders does not also need to be "simple, nontechnical, illustrated if possible, and attractive in appearance"? Is there any reason why a report cannot meet all of these standards and also be dignified? A very large corporation last year submitted one somewhat conventional report to its 250,000 stockholders and a different, simplified report to its 200,000 employees. Is it necessarily true that the general level of intelligence is higher among those stockholders than among those employees? The officers of that corporation evidently thought so. What is equally important, they gave evidence that they thought so. They made it possible for the employees to be told by some clever agitator that the company treated them as the mental inferiors of the stockholders, and gave them a kindergarten edition of the report! Another consideration is the possible suspicion that the "special" report for employees contains information different from that given the stockholders. If both reports contain the same facts, tell the same story, why not make them one report?

There are not a large number of corporations which give annual reports to employees, probably not 10 per cent of the companies whose stocks or bonds are listed. The majority of reports to employees are special reports, different from the reports to stockholders. At this early stage in the development of the custom, the fact that most companies issue special reports to employees is not evidence of the correctness of that plan. From actual inspection, it appears that many of these corporations would have done a better job if they had sent the employee report to the stockholders and the stockholders report to the museum.

A difficult problem exists where large numbers of employees are of foreign birth and are known to be unable to read English. It is not uncommon in Quebec for an annual report to be printed in parallel columns of English and French. In a large city with large foreign-speaking elements there are usually newspapers in the respective languages. If my payroll included five thousand Lithuanians, I think I should prepare a report which the average American worker (and stockholder) could read and pay the local Lithuanian newspaper to print it in Lithuanian! Where no language difficulty exists it seems to me unsound to assume a lower level of intelligence among employees than among stockholders.

Leaving the question whether one report or two are used, what should be in the report to employees? How should they get it? What results should follow?

Obviously the report should contain all the facts which appear in a well-presented balance sheet and profit-and-loss account. The usual accounting terms should be translated into words the employee and the stockholder can readily understand. Assets can be described as things owned by us. Gross income from sales can be identified as money received or to be received from goods or services sold. Accounts receivable can be called money owing to us. Liabilities can be money we owe. Most important, reserves, surplus, and capital can be explained as what they really are.

Besides the facts normally revealed or concealed in the balance sheet and profit-and-loss account, the report should contain some information as to how the results were accomplished. This can be and probably should be done in three ways.

The first is by simple, frank textual statements. "We were unable to sell any of our goods in Europe this year on account of the war. In the previous year, we sold in Europe $50,000 worth of mousetraps, and $60,000 worth of shoelaces. To try to make up for the loss of this business, we sent three men to South America. They were able to sell $30,000 worth of mousetraps there but found that people do not use shoelaces. However, they found that there was a good sale for butterfly nets. We spent $10,000 for special machines to make these nets. We sold $40,000 worth of them, and expect that next year we will sell $80,000 worth. If we do, we shall then have $110,000 worth of sales in South America instead of the $80,000 worth we formerly sold in Europe."

The second way is by including some tables of figures which concern neither assets and liabilities nor profit and loss, tables we call "statistical." Readable tables can be presented to list facts about numbers of employees, quantities of various materials purchased, sales by classes of goods, or by location, taxes for successive years, numbers of stockholders, and numerous other facts that have meaning.

The third way is by means of graphs, charts, or pictures. So many good books on the use of such illustrations and so many good examples of their use are available that they need no description here. But because I have seen some which have caused me internal pain, I take this opportunity to express a plea: Let the charts be simple enough to show one fact each and show it clearly, and let the pictures and pictographs be dignified enough to avoid competition with the Sunday colored comics!

Many of the best reports select one element of the business as material for a feature story in the annual report each year. A new oil field opened by the company, a new product, a new research laboratory, a new retirement plan—each of these has been given excellent treatment in the report of some company. Such a feature story invites the use of proper illustrations and gives life and action to the report.

Finally, not as content but as the carrier of subject matter, the report should use color where discretion permits. It should use paper which signifies respect for the reader. It should use type which shows consideration for his comfort.

How should employees get the report? Both experience and logic will say *not* by general distribution in the plant. If the report is to go indiscriminately to every employee, at least it should go to each as a person. If it is worth giving to him, it is worth mailing to him at home. Many of the values discussed under the techniques of direct mailing are added to the annual report which reaches the home of the employee.

But should the report go to all employees? Clearly there is no case to be made for the selection of certain employees to receive the report, that is, no case for selection of these by the employer. But is there an automatic selection which will enhance the value of the report to those who do receive it?

If the report is offered to all employees, there will be a number who will not request copies. But, similarly, if the report is given to all employees, there will be a number who will not read it—even if it is mailed to their homes. If it is offered, there is a reasonable hope that those who are interested enough to request copies will read them. Of course, no adequate research has yet been possible; but there is logic to support the belief that the final result will be at least as good if 50 per cent of the employees ask for the report and read it as it will be if all the employees receive it without expressing any wish for it.

One of the employee-relations values in connection with the annual report is the knowledge of the employees that they can get the report. Offering the report accomplishes this.

It should be recognized that if the report is offered instead of given, it is almost essential that it be the same annual report which goes to stockholders. That is the report and information which the employee should know he *can* get. If it is a special "report to employees," there seems to be no logical course but to give the report to all employees.

Several methods may be used together or as alternatives for offering the report. A notice on bulletin boards may tell the employee that he can get a copy by asking the personnel officer, or his foreman, supervisor, or superintendent. A request card may be put in his hands, by which he can make advance request for a copy. Perhaps because it is easier, perhaps because it is more private, the latter method seems in actual tests to bring substantially higher percentages of requests.

What results should follow the giving of the annual report to employees, either indiscriminately or on request, either the stockholders' report or a special report?

No spectacular and immediate results can be expected,

that is, unless there is something startling in the report itself. But one result can be seen. The employees know that they can get the report; they can find out some of the things they have not known before.

There is no basis for expecting that the employees will now understand the position of the company as to finances, markets, and materials. There is no reason to expect that the best-presented annual report of the best-managed corporation will produce understanding judgment in the mind of every employee and create in him a new enthusiasm for his work, his company, and his boss and a conscious affiliation with the free-enterprise system.

But there is one result which can be expected, which can be seen and measured, and which should be hoped for above all else. The employees—this one, that one, another one—can be expected to ask questions. If even 5 per cent of the employees can be known to have asked a question of anyone, any question prompted by something in the annual report, the result is beneficial for months to come.

If the report is made readable and understandable, if employees know that they can get it, if some or many of them ask for it, and a few of them ask questions about it, we are starting along the road toward understanding. But how far we go on the road depends on what we do with those questions: whether or not we answer them sincerely, whom we select to do the answering, and how we enlarge the actual question into a consideration of many related pieces of information. In other chapters I record my declaration of faith in the line organization as the ideal agency to use this opportunity.

XIV

THE HOUSE ORGAN

Different types of publications are classed as house organs by their publishers. Probably the most common meaning is that of a periodical publication by a business or industrial institution designed for circulation among those who are members of the organization, that is, the employees. However, the name "house organ" is frequently applied to a publication circulated to the customers or clients of the business institution. And some corporations publish periodicals which they call house organs for circulation to their stockholders.

In relation to sharing information with employees, our interest is in the house organ designed for employees. However, we must not omit reference to the very effective use which can be made of magazines published for customers or stockholders. When such publications reach employees they have a certain "spice" which does not attach to the same material obviously directed at employees. It is something akin to reading somebody else's mail. The serious value may be chiefly in the fact that statements to customers or stockholders are looked upon by employees as more reliable than any effort of "the company" to pass out propaganda to the employees themselves.

This incidental value of customer and stockholder house organs is important to our main subject, and will be referred to again. But here we concentrate on the subject of employee house organs.

These are of many kinds, classified according to their characteristics. They may be departmental, plant-wide, or company-wide in the case of a widely scattered enterprise. They may be edited by employees, even published by employees. They may be edited by some staff agency high up in the company organization. They may be edited by management, with contributions or correspondence supplied by employees. They may be of the "gossip" variety, devoted chiefly to marriages, births, vacations, and athletic activities. They may be nearly filled with technical articles or may have only an occasional technical article included. They may be printed cheaply, planned to be read quickly and thrown away —the newspaper variety. Or they may be dignified and more expensive, more beautiful, in the hope that they will be kept—the magazine variety, sometimes even a real souvenir or keepsake.

While every variety of employee house organ must be considered in sharing information with employees, not all varieties are equally effective. The style which fits one phase of the program does not fit another. Above all, the particular variety in use is more likely to be the result of the personal aptitudes and tastes of those who control it than the result of a conscious study of method and medium. Let us look at some of the different types, strictly in the light of their functions in our program.

First we consider one having these features: It is gossipy or newsy, with lots of names, personalities, events. It is printed to be read and thrown away. If it is a good one of its kind, it has a liberal quantity of pictures. If it serves an enterprise widely scattered, it has a section for each plant; if it serves a single establishment, it has a section for each main department. Probably it has one or two editorials about the enterprise in general. It may carry, as if by concession of privilege, an occasional letter from the manager or president. In season, it will present letters from employees who are away on trips.

What does this kind of house organ do, in the program of sharing information with employees? How well does it do it? What are its dangers or disadvantages?

The best thing this kind of a house organ can do in our program is to build "company-consciousness," a feeling of belonging, the reaction we call *esprit de corps* or comradeship. By its influence the messenger boy can be led to feel that he has a community of interest with the purchasing agent, the sales manager can feel a good democratic chagrin because the janitor's fish was larger than his own. A substitute is provided for actual personal contact and acquaintance with employees in other departments or plants. Some grasp of the size of the organization can be given.

Such a house organ can reflect a feeling of comradeship and democracy. It can express and foster such a feeling. It cannot create it if the feeling does not exist in the daily life of the organization. But it can picture and dramatize a sense of contact which has actually been built on a foundation of real contact.

It has disadvantages. It must be consistent in its character, always personal, always with employee flavor, always newsy and spontaneous. The occasional technical article seems out of place unless the man who wrote it is featured and is interesting as a person. The occasional letter from the president is appropriate only if it is written to or about a person who in his own right is entitled to mention. The article about the new product fits the picture only if it is written, preferably as an account of personal experience, by someone whose name has already appeared in the news.

It has dangers, too. In a reasonably large company or plant, it cannot report all the marriages, all the births, all the hunting trips, all the interesting personal news. Even in the course of a year, it can hardly manage to mention every employee at least once. When your name or mine has been left out, we feel some disappointment. When Joe Doakes and his wife have their pictures published, leaving for Niagara, we resent the fact that our trip to Alaska was not even mentioned. In fact, we feel the opposite of a sense of comradeship and democracy. We lose a little confidence in the editorial staff and even suspect that the publication plays favorites.

Turning to a radically different type of house organ, let us appraise it in terms of the same values. This time it is frankly a communication from management to employees. Instead of relying on names and news and pictures of employees, to get itself read, it seeks to be attractive in appearance—has good paper, pleasing format, plenty of color. It is printed to be taken home and kept. It features persons only when an action or achievement is an expression of company tradition or character: an act of heroism by a member of a safety committee which expresses a tradition of interest in safety; or the completion of fifty years of service, which reflects the stability of the enterprise and its practice of retaining its employees. It leans toward direct discussion and explanation of the various activities and functions of the company: the safety program, research, sales, plant expansions, new products. It is edited "at the top" and makes no show of originating with the rank and file.

What can this kind of house organ do, in our program of sharing information with employees?

Obviously, if it exists at all, it is part and parcel of the program. Without apology, it can carry the information which is most fundamental. It can build *esprit de corps* not by leading employees to feel acquainted with each other but by acquainting them with the broad activities and basic character of the business. However, like the gossipy house organ, it can build this spirit but cannot create it. There must be a foundation of company character which is fit to be portrayed. But by its successive presentation of functions and policies, it can help to crystallize the understanding of them. When it pictures the policy of continuity of employment, dramatized by Lars Olson's fiftieth anniversary, that policy becomes a little clearer, a little firmer, in the mind of every company agent who deals with employment.

It has disadvantages. It must bid high for the employee's interest or attention. Because it does not offer him the chance to read his own name or see his own picture, it must overcome his indifference or it will never be read. Its front cover must attract his eye by form and color. Its particular subject titles must be worded so as to call on him for attention, create his desire to see the stories inside. Its printing, illustrations, size, frequency of publication, language, and every other detail must be studied and planned with great care. It has to win its way into his interest and reading against a natural indifference.

And it has dangers, too. If it sways even a little in the direction of giving him ready-made thoughts and opinions, instead of facts from which he can form opinions, it will create resentment and injure morale. If it makes any appeal to him to think this or do that, it is classed as propaganda in the interest of the bosses.

Reference has been made to the type of house organ addressed to customers or stockholders, basically prepared for their information, and circulated to employees sometimes as an afterthought, sometimes as part of a regular program. Some of the best jobs of sharing information with employees have been done through this type of publication. Its presentation to employees can be frank and natural. For instance:

1. "This history of our company was prepared for our stockholders. It has proved so interesting that we have arranged for enough extra copies to supply each of the employees. It not only tells the story of your company but contains some pictures which you may want and which have not been published anywhere else."
2. "This booklet was prepared to introduce our new Lifetime Polish to our dealers and customers. It tells the story of this achievement of our Research Laboratory so well that we want everyone who has a part in the enterprise to see it, not only so that he will know the story, but so that he will know how we are trying to get the new product before the public. We believe this is a field for bigger sales, making more and better jobs."

Experience indicates that such methods of presenting information are appreciated by employees. Partly this must be due to satisfaction in the mere knowledge that they are getting something which was prepared for the stockholders or customers. This is related to what is said elsewhere about the distribution of the annual report. But partly also it may be due to the fact that such a publication is likely to be good by every standard. Intelligent management does not give a publication to customers or stockholders unless it has been carefully prepared, designed, and printed.

An interesting illustration reversing this procedure is that of a very successful corporation which publishes one of the most beautiful and effective employee house organs in America—and then also distributes it to customers and prospective customers. It becomes an outstandingly good medium of sales promotion!

We might picture several other distinct types of house organs. Of every one which is good in its class we should conclude that it can do something in a program of sharing information with employees, that it has some disadvantages, and that it has some positive dangers. Still confessing that generalizations are unsound, we do suggest a general attitude toward the medium of the employee house organ:

If it is good, if it does its job well, overcomes its disadvantages and avoids its dangers, it is not at best the whole of the program.

If it does the best possible job, the result is valuable beyond measure, but only as a preparation for the real job of sharing information with employees.

Let us assume again an especially successful issue of the second type of house organ we described, the issue which told of the completion of fifty years of service by Lars Olson. How are we to know whether or not the results are good, whether or not the story was read and its real meaning comprehended? Not by the number of letters received from employee readers;

these will be few at best. Not by the number of comments which wives of employees make to the manager's wife. Not by the pride and enthusiasm of Lars himself. The real measure will be the amount of curiosity stimulated in the minds of employees and revealed by them. If the job was well done, foremen and supervisors will be answering questions for weeks to come. Is Lars going to retire? Will he get a pension? Is he the oldest employee in years of age? How many employees have worked here forty-five years? Forty years? Who will be the next fifty-year man? What is the average age of all the employees? Were any of them over forty when they were hired? How come Lars hasn't been promoted lots farther? Doesn't seniority count much?

The best job of the best house organ of this type is to stir up interest in its subject, and induce employees to ask questions. If the basic relationship is right, those questions will come to foremen and supervisors. If our program of sharing information with employees has been wisely planned, the foreman or supervisor will know it.

XV

THE HANDBOOK

The name "handbook" is applied to a variety of publications or compilations which may seem to have very few common characteristics. In its adaptation for distribution to employees by employers, however, it is usually found to be similar in such matters as size, permanence, circulation, and method of use and different in title, content, and purpose. For our discussion we may think of it as a booklet small enough to be carried in the pocket, one which is designed for reasonable life or permanence but is subject to occasional revision, one which is uniformly supplied to all employees of a company, an establishment, or a department, and one which is designed for ready and frequent reference. But we must also think of it as varying in title through a range which includes manual, rule book, guide, and statement of policy or procedure; as varying in content from a printed speech by the company president to a detailed mass of directions as to clothing, conduct, and causes for immediate discharge; and as varying in purpose from a desire to equip employees to deal effectively with customers to a desire to impress employees with the requirements of their jobs.

Within these limitations, these similarities and variations, it presents one of the most effective means yet devised for sharing information with employees. Like every other specific medium, it is incapable of doing the whole job. But to a greater extent than most others it can be made to meet the fundamental needs.

It can be so planned as to be a natural factor in the relation between employer and employee, one which serves an obvious purpose directly related to the daily life interest of the employee. It may in a large establishment, furnish him with information which is clearly needed in his conduct as a member of the organization, information about location of various facilities such as rest rooms, smoking rooms, supply rooms. In a plant of any size it can anticipate his questions on such matters as advances on pay, available insurance opportunities, and credit union facilities. In short, it can present information which is so obviously needed by him that its presentation in any form is natural and no apology need be made for the selection of the handbook form.

At first glance the handbook may not seem to be a gradual and continuing method of sharing information with employees. It seems to be a once-and-for-all presentation of its contents. However, any booklet of the type we are discussing is designed for continuous or at least repeated reference. Its form must not suggest that it is something to be read once and thrown away. If it is the simplest, crudest compilation of company rules, the average employee will keep it available somewhere and will probably have occasion to look at it, some time, for months after he first receives it. Most of the types of handbook for employees are subject to periodical revision, probably not more than once in a year, but still furnishing an occasion to call in an old issue and substitute a new one. To some extent, the repeated references to the booklet, as information is needed by the employee on specific subjects, will make it both a gradual and a continuing medium.

The handbook device can qualify completely on the requirement that it must permeate the whole organization. In its original preparation, or in its periodical revision, there is an opportunity to enlist the participation of foremen or supervisors and of employee committees dealing with safety, credit unions, or baseball teams. The group so enlisted will be actively aware of the contents of the booklet, conscious of the responsibility which results from having been consulted, and ready to explain and elaborate the contents for their fellow workers. The subsequent distribution of the booklet will carry it to all the employees in the unit concerned. Because its circulation is complete and its contents are of common interest, it can permeate the organization more completely than most other carriers of information.

Leaving temporarily the question of content and purpose, we may point out important factors of physical form and appearance of handbooks for employees. The suggestion that the booklet is something to be kept for future reference can be destroyed by an appearance of being "flimsy." A booklet which is not accorded the consideration by the employer which would involve good paper, good printing, and a substantial and durable cover cannot win the consideration of an employee which would lead him to try to retain it for future use.

The cover is of special importance, not only for its durability and its suggestion of value, but also for its appropriateness to the kind of establishment. In a department store, a bank, or an insurance office, the cover can be light and attractive in color. In a machine shop, it should be of such a color that the first touch of black and greasy fingers will not make it look ready for the waste can. If the booklet is likely to be carried around by a salesman, an electrical lineman, or an installment collector, the cover should be one which will endure the rubbing and bending of life in a pocket.

The printing on the outside of the cover deserves to be considered in connection with appearance as well as in connection with content and purpose. The title must describe intelligently what is inside the booklet, but it can also contribute to interest in reading and in retaining the booklet. It is probably much more effective to print on the cover the words "Information for Employees of the Jones Company" than the words "Rules for Employees of the Jones Company."

A variation which has been found effective is an exposed title which will suggest that the contents are not intended for the world at large, but are a part of the special relationship which exists between the employer and the employees. To mark the handbook "CONFIDENTIAL" is rarely justifiable. If it does contain information which obviously should not be told the outsiders, there is a reason for calling it confidential; but it is difficult to imagine information of this kind which would appear in any printed handbook. On the other hand, it may be proper and natural to use such a title as "Jones Company—Information for Employees Only." These words convey a suggestion of privacy, which has some tendency to create interest in advance. We have suggested elsewhere that some facts which should be known to the man in the plant but not the man in the street can actually be best protected by sharing them with employees—provided the employees can also see the reasons why the neighbor or the customer or the competitor should not have the information at the same time. The handbook of "Information for Employees Only" seems to offer an excellent medium for developing this consciousness.

A frequent function of the handbook of information for employees is to indicate, directly or indirectly, certain specific information which employees may want and can get but which is not actually included in the handbook. For instance, the booklet may contain a general description of the group-insurance opportunities available to the employee but not the detailed instruction as to application methods, premium rates, exact benefits, and so forth. This leads up to the statement that full information can be obtained by consulting such-and-such a person or department. Reference may be made to the fact that employees have organized, and are operating, a credit union. Such details as unit share prices, required payments, dividend rates, how to join, conditions for getting loans, interest rates, etc., are not likely to appear. In fact, they probably should not appear in a booklet published by the employer. But the information can well be given that the credit union office is located at a given place and is open from three to five every afternoon.

Probably most valuable in this function is the opportunity to introduce subject matter on which more details are likely to be wanted and yet without reference to any staff supervisor or office from which these details can be learned. If these references to the subject matter itself lead the employee to consult his immediate supervisor, well—there is no greater value than this. Whether he asks the supervisor for the information or asks him where to get the information, the result is equally valuable.

Quite different in form is a handbook of "Information for Visitors" which is sometimes issued in a separate edition designated to indicate in some way that it is a special issue for employees but with the clear inference that it is for the use of employees in supplying information to visitors. Many public utility companies have, and use, an exceptional opportunity to share information with employees in a similar way. Their employees contact the customers or consumers. Therefore it is most natural to supply such a handbook to employees, not because they need or do not supposedly have the information, but because both they and their management want the facts passed on to customers.

Information offered for such a purpose is psychologically more acceptable to any of us than that which is offered with the implication that we ourselves should know something which we do not know. Further, the enlistment in the task of passing on information to visitors, customers, or the public causes us to know the particular facts actively instead of passively.

Leaving the discussion of handbooks which convey information of the kinds suggested, good use has been made by many employers, large and small, of a booklet completely devoted to a statement of company policy in relation to employees. The evolution of such booklet in one large company is interesting, and, while not the usual process, is by no means unique.

This evolution covered a period of several years. The first step was that of reducing to writing the policies which had actually evolved and were actually in effect. Incidentally, this step took some two years, I was told. The next step was the confidential distribution of this statement to nearly a hundred branch managers. The next step was a revision of the statement in co-operation with these managers, over a period of some three years. Then followed the informal presentation of the confidential statement to line supervisors, sometimes by "lending" the confidential copies, sometimes by presenting the contents, a portion at a time, in group meetings.

Finally, the supervisors themselves, down to the direct work supervisors, were invited to recommend revisions. With these revisions installed, the "policy" was printed in an attractive form and a copy was supplied to every line supervisor. The cover imprint showed clearly that it was intended for supervisors only. Some of the higher line executives now expressed the opinion that understanding will be greatly enhanced if wage earners themselves can generally "get hold" of copies—not as a statement intended for them but as a revelation of how the attitudes of supervisors toward workers are shaped and what the real policy is which guides the supervisors in their dealings with workers.

Not all the types of information which employers wish to share with employees can be effectively shared through the medium of the handbook. Not all of them can use a booklet which is small, semipermanent, widely distributed, and usable for ready and repeated reference. We have suggested only the general types of information which can well be supplied in this form. Primarily this is information for the actual guidance of employees. Slightly removed is a catalogue of information for visitors or customers; actually it is for the guidance of the employee in his contacts or dealings with these outsiders. Perhaps the "company policy" booklet can be classed as being for the guidance of supervisors in their dealings with employees; when it is distributed to all employees, it may guide them in checking their own daily experiences to see that the policies are being applied.

Occasionally a company which has an interesting history has presented that in the form of a handbook. Sometimes this is effective in the sense of supplying information which employees will use in contacts with outsiders; this makes the history handbook a reference text. In other cases, it achieves permanence by the attractiveness or beauty of its form, becoming a worth-while souvenir. One progressive organization published a history of the city in which it operated so attractive that it became a souvenir for both employees and public and seems to have inspired pride in employees for the part which "their" enterprise had played in the history. However, the souvenir idea is a departure from our concept of the handbook as being essentially informative and adaptable for repeated reference.

One of the worst mistakes in the use of the handbook idea has been the issuance of such a booklet to present the story of a labor dispute between the company and the employees, or rather, between the company and some agency which the company management believes represents the employees improperly. Whether such a booklet tries to discredit the representatives or to argue with the employees themselves, it is usually an example of both bad taste and bad judgment. Bad taste may be a matter of opinion. The criticism of bad judgment is more nearly capable of proof. The attempt to restore understanding by means of a printed message is likely to fail when misunderstanding has resulted from conversation, argument, and daily-work relationships; the restoration needs a deeper foundation than a booklet presenting the management's view. If understanding is to be achieved eventually, so constructive a medium as the handbook should not be discredited by use as a weapon in the controversy.

Quite immune to such criticism is the presentation of such

material as a union agreement which has been negotiated and which has become the constitution of the organized relations within the enterprise. The publication of such an agreement in handbook form fits exactly the standards of a good handbook. It can always be prepared in the appropriate size. It is semipermanent, that is, it is the basis of relations for a fixed period. It is subject to general distribution. And certainly it is intended for ready and frequent reference. Constructively it can definitely build for understanding. Whether it is an old agreement renewed or an agreement for the first time, whether reached amicably or after severe conflict, its possession by every employee affected is important. However, the value can be gotten only by wise preparation. The action of an employer in printing and distributing such an agreement without discussion or co-operation with the officers of the union or unions concerned carries a suggestion of hostility. The inclusion of the union representatives in planning, designing, and presenting the publication almost automatically wins for the employer the credit for a sincere act of co-operation.

Subject matter such as a financial statement, a "newsy" story of current happenings, the announcement of a new branch, a new product or new service cannot ordinarily be presented in handbook form. An exception would be the use of a reference handbook for employees who should engage in the promotion of a new product or new service. For most such classes of subject matter, however, more effective use can be made of other media such as the souvenir magazine, the house organ, or the direct-mail letter.

When it is suitable, when it is well used, the handbook is superior to most other media. Its superiority is in the most important function of prompting closer contact with and directing questions to the "always best" medium for sharing information with employees—the line supervisor.

XVI

DIRECT MAIL

The term "direct mail" describes in general the method of delivering a communication. In our study of sharing information with employees it therefore includes the procedure of mailing any piece of information to each employee, or each member of a selected group of employees. It presumes that the mailing address used is his home address, not his working address, in care of the employer. It could include the house organ, a reprint of a newspaper or magazine article, or a piece of sales-advertising material, each mailed to the employee at his home.

Depending on immediate conditions of time, place, and attitudes, direct mailing probably adds to the effectiveness of any piece of printed or written information offered to employees. It seems to have a particular appropriateness when applied to the annual report of a corporation. On the face of the appraisal, this method of delivery seems to emphasize the importance and value of the article which is mailed. It advertises the fact that the employer considers the material to be of sufficient value to justify him in paying postage on it. The assumption is that the recipient will accordingly consider it of sufficient value to take the time to read it.

When this objective is important in the mind of the employer, he will probably try to select his direct-mail material in such a way that it will logically require first-class postage. If the material arrives in an unsealed envelope, it competes for attention with a flood of similarly delivered material. There is no need to cite even a few examples of the useless, uninteresting, and even annoying unsealed communications which we all receive and most of which we do not read.

Surely we do not want a communication important enough to be mailed to our employees to go directly into the fire. It may do just that if it arrives unsealed and looks just about as important and personal as the circular which arrived yesterday soliciting a contribution for the Society for the Protection of Perishing Penguins.

Of course, the desirability of first-class postage does not exist equally in the case of direct-mail matter which is bulky and which has the appearance which will attract attention in its own right. A case in point is the annual report of the corporation. If this is a document of twelve or more pages, well printed on good paper, and with a well-planned cover, it has a good chance to be examined if it arrives in an open-end envelope.

In addition to attesting the importance of the material, direct mailing seems to suggest something of a personal element. The individuality of the employee is respected when an envelope is addressed to him. This is true even if the addressing machine is used. But just as first-class mailing increases the impression of the importance of the material, so does individual addressing increase the sense of respect for the person who receives it. If the desire to share a piece of information with employees justifies its careful preparation and typing or printing, it probably justifies the expense of first-class mailing. It may fully justify an additional cost of two or three cents per employee for hand addressing.

Both these expenses need to be considered in the light of what may result from saving half the postage cost or two-thirds of the addressing cost. We cannot surely determine whether or not first-class postage will lead the employee to value the material sufficiently to read it or if individual addressing does or does not appeal to him as a courteous gesture inducing friendliness before he opens the envelope. But we can decide whether unsealed delivery and machine addressing will brand the material as cheap and impersonal. If there is a chance of this result, we may well hesitate to save the difference and thus reduce the effectiveness of our whole story.

A third natural advantage of direct mailing of information is that, in the case of a married employee, we know it reaches the home. Of course, a beautiful magazine or an automatically interesting report, "handed out" at the plant, is likely to be carried home and shown to wife or mother or sons. But not all our information can be presented in attractive magazine form and be automatically interesting. When we can feel sure that any piece of material gets into the family circle, we are much closer to the ideal result of stimulating conversation and interest, much surer of questions coming back next day, on the job, and thus opening up the ultimate channel for sharing information and moving toward understanding.

All the foregoing relates to the method of delivery of any one of many possible media of sharing information with employees. There is a medium different from any which we have discussed and which has a particular claim on the name of direct mail. This medium is the special letter prepared, and obviously prepared, for the sole purpose of being mailed to the employee. It is essentially a letter to the employee, whether printed, typed, or produced in facsimile, and whether containing mere comments on events and problems or reports of business results for definite periods.

Direct mail, in this sense of the word, seems to be the best available substitute for the personal interview when the personal interview is impractical. It is an attractive medium in the following circumstances: (1) where it is desired to convey the same information to a large number of employees at the same time; (2) where it is important to convey the information in precise form so as to avoid, as far as possible, the danger of having it misquoted; (3) where it is desired to give to the message the value of sponsorship or authorship by a certain individual, such as the president of the company, who therefore signs the letter.

Reference should be made to the practice of some companies who have made the letter from the president to the employees a regular and periodical part of the structure of their employee relations. One such company, employing approximately five hundred, has had outstanding success with this medium. The monthly letter from the president has become a tradition over a period of years. It carries certain information regularly and is practically a monthly report of the business. It reports production, sales, and orders received. In addition it always discusses some information of strictly current interest. It has proved itself a useful link in the chain of understanding.

The sudden launching of such a medium as a "monthly letter from the president" is probably unwise. The announcement that the employee is to expect such a letter each month "from now on" is likely to prove embarrassing. No employer can embark on the permanent use of this or any other conventional medium of sharing information with employees and feel sure that such a medium is a wise or useful one for his particular organization. In the company cited above, it has proved itself a good medium. But that result has not depended on the monthly letter alone. The letter has been acceptable because it fits in with all other elements of the employee relations of the company. It has been effective because the president actually prepares it himself, expresses himself in it, and considers it a definite part of his job.

For the employer who has not used it, and who believes that the direct-mail letter will build understanding with his employees, the launching should be modest and not irrevocable. Some proper occasion will present itself, some subject which will impress the employee reader as a natural topic about which the president should write a letter. It will be a subject of such nature that there will be no surprise at the letter being written, and equally no surprise if no more letters are received, at least for several months.

To serve this purpose, it is obvious that such a subject as the month's production or sales, or any other subject which is part of the story of every month, will not be suitable. On the other hand, if production or sales for the month represent an all-time record, that may justify a letter from the president. If that record is not equaled, or is merely equaled, during the three following months, no follow-up letter is expected. But if, in the second or fourth following month, a new high record is achieved, that is a natural occasion for another letter.

The participation of the company in the national defense program is a natural, almost a compelling subject for direct information to employees. A direct-mail letter on this topic can usually carry some information not publicly known and can thereby give the employee a proper consciousness of the fact that he is trusted and is responsible for a trust.

The introduction of a new product, if the product is planned to become important in the program of production or of sales, qualifies as a suitable occasion for a first direct-mail letter to employees. If the offering of the new item is accompanied by an advertising campaign, some piece of the advertising copy may well be enclosed. If the advertising campaign is planned for three months or six months, the first letter to employees may properly promise a future letter which will report on the results. This makes no commitment to an unending series of letters from the president at regular intervals, "from now on."

Any important event which is truly news gives an equally appropriate occasion for a first direct-mail letter or for a letter which follows one or many others. It is acceptable and effective procedure to inform employees, by such a letter, of the undertaking to build a new plant, or the selection of a new president or manager, or the acquisition of a new source of supply or line of merchandise, or the entering of a new foreign market. One important point is that such a letter must not tell the employee merely the same things he can learn or has learned from the newspaper. It must either tell him the same story before the newspaper tells it, or it must tell him some significant facts in addition to those appearing in the newspaper story.

There are some things which the direct-mail letter must never do. Most of them are things which no vehicle of information should ever do. But because the direct-mail letter is direct, because it is personal, and because it carries the responsibility of its author, it is one medium which must particularly avoid the dangers of these mistakes.

Like all other media, it must not be used to scold or complain. Justifiable causes for complaint by an employer are the actions — or the inactions — of certain individual employees. Good management can usually reach those responsible without "crying on the shoulder" of every employee, either through a bulletin on the board or a letter in the mail.

The direct-mail letter can never be wisely or effectively used to tell the employee how well he is treated by the management nor how much the management wants to do for him if he will only co-operate. It should avoid, as carefully as should any other medium, the attempt to give him conclusions and opinions instead of facts, or to influence directly his own political conclusions and actions.

A popular use of the direct-mail medium in recent years has been for printed material supplied by outside agencies. Some of these agencies are associations of industrialists, business men, or individuals interested in a particular interpretation of the American philosophy. Some are private commercial ventures, selling mailing material in wholesale lots.

In general the material supplied by private publishers is superior to that of the nonprofit associations. None of the printed matter deals with facts about a particular employer or enterprise. It is nevertheless entitled to be classed as information. It frequently presents, in excellent manner, the important facts about American economics, standards of living, protection of personal liberties, and dangers of subversion. Although there are exceptions, most of the material of this type is free from political propaganda. Some employers purchase quantities of brief weekly "releases" and mail them to all employees or selected groups. Others supply mailing lists to the publishing agency, pay the required price, and arrange for the weekly releases to be mailed directly to the employees from the headquarters of the publisher.

There is room for argument as to the effectiveness of any such stereotyped direct-mail matter. There are cases showing that it has built understanding. But it is not a process of sharing information with employees in the sense of objective facts supplied by the employer directly. It is outside the strict limits of the program we are discussing.

One use has been made of the direct-mail letter which is contrary to good taste, contrary to good tactics, and possibly contrary to good citizenship. This is its use to by-pass a collective-bargaining committee or agent chosen to represent the employees. The direct-mail communication in such cases may be utterly truthful and factual, free from argument or attempted interpretation. But the mere issuance of it is an influence against understanding, not toward understanding.

An actual instance dramatizes this use of the direct-mail letter. Several other channels could have been used to convey the same information, with equally bad results; but the virtues of the direct-mail plan led to its selection as ideal, in the mind of the employer concerned. After prolonged negotiations between this employer and a committee representing a clear majority of his employees, no agreement was in sight on wages, working conditions, and union status. Without prior announcement to the union committee, the employer mailed directly to each employee a document carrying the story of the negotiations up to date. It can be assumed that the document was truthful and factual, although it is easily possible that the employer was more successful in restating his own pronouncements than in restating the arguments, demands, or pronouncements of the committee. Possibly the right of free speech permitted the employer to lay these facts before each of his employees. That is a question for experts in the newer phases of labor law to discuss. Some of them will assert that he departed from required procedures of collective bargaining by going past the authorized representatives to the employees as individuals. That is merely a question whether or not the action was contrary to good citizenship. In any case, the act had unfortunate implications.

The first implication of this action was the employer's belief that the committee was not fully or truthfully reporting the negotiations to the employees. If he had no doubt on this question, he could have had no reason to try to do that reporting job himself—particularly to do it without notice to the committee.

The second implication was that he hoped the employees would do something about it, that they might instruct their committee to modify its demands, to accept some of the employer's proposals which he had thus reported—they might even repudiate and displace the committee or refuse to follow its leadership if it called on them to strike.

As a matter of fact, the employees did none of these apparently hoped-for things. They supported the committee. The committee lost all sense of progress toward understanding with the employer who had thus by-passed them. The early consequence was, not understanding, but an unfortunate strike which was the evidence of both chronic and acute misunderstanding.

Used appropriately as to time and subject matter, the direct-mail letter can be one of the most effective media for sharing information with employees and building toward understanding. Used inappropriately, it can be extremely harmful.

At its best, it must be one feature of a whole way of life which makes for understanding. If not harmful, it will at least be ineffective if the basic attitude of the employer is not conducive to understanding. It will be ineffective if it is relied upon to do the whole job of conveying information, if it is not supported by a frank, informed channel of information which flows through the entire line organization from president to foreman.

At its best, it will convey some limited information and will demonstrate without declaring that employees are welcome to information. The good result will be the same as that of any other medium—interest, confidence, freedom of questions carried to the line supervisors. To a greater degree than most other media, it will produce interest and generate questions at home, in the most important area of employee understanding.

XVII

CIVIC GROUP MEETINGS

The obvious fact about civic group meetings as a channel for sharing information with employees is that the employees are not in the usual civic group meeting. Even when this fact is conceded, we cannot disregard such groups as an important link in a full program.

By civic groups we mean no special selection, but the whole circle of such organizations. This includes primarily the usual service clubs. In addition, it includes every group which meets, regularly or occasionally, to listen to speakers who discuss subjects of civic interest. Within this broad definition would fall luncheon or dinner meetings of the Chamber of Commerce or commercial clubs. Also there would be some fraternal organizations holding similar meetings, parent-teacher groups, Red Cross chapter meetings, church brotherhoods, women's clubs, groups of educators or social workers, groups of government employees concerned with safety or social security, taxpayers' leagues, granges and other farmer organizations, and possibly some trade or professional groups such as merchants, doctors, dentists, ministers.

To justify this broad and varied list we must agree on some definition of "subjects of civic interest." Naturally we include the usual subjects of public civic improvements such as streets, lights, water, sewers, parks, playgrounds, schools, and all phases of public safety, health, and welfare. We include also the wide range of semipublic problems which have to do with making "our city" or "our community" a better and more interesting place in which to live. This range extends in all directions, both inside and outside the corporate limits of the town or city.

It is a subject of civic interest that a thousand or thirty thousand people, living somewhere else, have invested their money in the industries of our community, that as stockholders they are concerned with the steady and efficient operation of our plants and businesses. It is a subject of civic interest that one-third or one-half of our population is supported directly by this or that industry. It is a subject of civic interest that a hundred or a thousand salesmen in a score of states are working to send orders to the mills or warehouses in our town, or that a thousand or a hundred thousand consumers are using the products or services of our local enterprises.

It is a matter of civic interest that the main mill in our town is first, fifth, or fifteenth in its industry; or that it pays a tenth or a half of the local taxes; or that its raw materials are adequate and safeguarded or their source is jeopardized by some foreign war development. The definition can thus be extended to great limits.

It is a subject of supreme civic interest that our plant, our workers, or our community have the opportunity to take a certain part in the war effort of the nation. It may be the production of guns or of gunny sacks. It may be the conversion of our sugar warehouse into storage space for medical supplies. It may be the sacrifice of our principal industry because its raw material is needed for the Navy, and the consequent displacement of the workers and their gradual transfer to defense industries. It may be the provision of housing for a thousand new workers who are coming to town to man the jobs in an expanding defense industry.

But, having broadly defined our groups, and even more broadly defined the subjects of civic interest, the fact remains that our employees are not in these groups or at best only a few of them are in a few of the groups. However, another fact has been demonstrated, sometimes painfully, to many employers. It is that the comments by speakers before these civic groups do find a way of reaching our employees.

What is the third fact, or set of facts, which may reconcile these two? Omitting the possibility that some of our employees are present in some of the groups, such as the church or fraternal gatherings, the answer seems to be in a series of indirect contacts. First, the wives, mothers, and sisters of some of our employees are certainly found in the parent-teacher groups. The teachers of the boys and girls of our employees are in these same groups and also in some of the educational and social-work groups. Second, the retailers, garage owners, doctors, dentists, and many others who hear the speaker at the service club or commercial club will be seeing and talking with some of our employees, perhaps later that day, or in the days soon after. Third, in the average industrial community the local paper will carry some report of what the speaker said at the noon meeting today or at the dinner meeting last night. Some of our employees or their wives will read these reports.

All these channels and contacts are indirect and inefficient as channels for supplying information to employees. But they are among the most effective means which can be imagined for creating an interest in the employee's mind, in other words for persuading him to "tune in" mentally on the wave length of any desired topic.

At some Friday night supper in the home of Gus Gorman, a machine operator at our mill or your mill, Gus Junior repeats what the teacher said that day in geography class. Perhaps it is that the local mill uses some steel alloy from Alaska, or glass from Slovakia, or wool from Australia. Perhaps it is that twelve hundred French workers in Marseilles before the war were making rayon out of pulp from the local mill, or that workers in a similar mill in some other country earn an average of 20 cents an hour as against 90 cents in the local mill—the teacher heard this fact from a recent speaker at some group meeting.

Or perhaps Mrs. Gus Gorman is the one who brings it up,

because she heard a speaker mention it at the parent-teacher meeting that day. Or perhaps the dentist mentioned it to her that afternoon, when she took little Betty to his office. He knew that Gus worked in the mill, and he had heard the fact from a speaker at the service club two days before.

If Gus already knew the particular fact, he probably knows a little more to add to the discussion. He is likely, also, to ask something more about it at the mill next day. If he did not know about it, he is almost sure to ask about it at the mill next day. In either case, it is likely that an interest or curiosity has been created in his mind—a desire for, or a willingness to receive, information on a particular subject, or related to that subject.

At this point we face one of the most critical tests of our readiness to share information with employees. The natural target for the question from Gus is the immediate supervisor, foreman, or straw boss. The channel may be blocked at this point if we have failed to create the free and willing contact relationship which prompts Gus to ask the boss. It may be blocked if Gus finds out—more surely, if he has previously found out—that the boss does not know the answers.

If this is a first occurrence, and the immediate supervisor does not know the answer, wisdom will prompt him to say so and to promise to try to find out. The "tuning in" process, the stimulation of interest and curiosity, has then done double duty. The supervisor, as well as Gus, is open for information.

In surveying the place of the civic group in the program of sharing information with employees, we discover two definite and positive tasks. One is to plan for facts to reach the civic group, facts which are significant, interesting, dramatic, and so simple and definite that they are still alive and accurate after having been relayed several times, perhaps from the lawyer to his secretary, from the secretary to her mother at home, from the mother to Mrs. Gus at the grocery store.

The second task is to see to it that the supervisor or foreman can meet the probable question from Gus with dignity and assurance. He must be ready to confirm, correct, or expound the item about which Gus may ask, or be able to secure the necessary confirmation or correction in short order. There is so much to be said about this task that a later chapter will be devoted to it. Our attention here is given to the first task—planning for stimulating, significant facts to reach the civic groups.

Surely the first step is an inventory of the groups concerned, in the community where our business establishment operates. The second is an inventory of our contacts with those groups through memberships. Related to this second step may be the need of creating or encouraging such contacts where they do not already exist.

Another book should be written about the duty and privilege of a business enterprise to be actively represented in the civic organizations such as we are discussing. The inventory which we now need to make involves a more delicate and immediate problem.

In any step toward sharing information with employees, we must avoid an invasion of those areas of life which lie outside the relation of employer and employee. We cannot respectably impose either inquisition or dictatorship on any member of our organization in relation to his civic activities. Therefore, we cannot start our inventory of contacts by placing a questionnaire before even our management representatives or supervisors, asking "To what service club do you belong? To what church brotherhood? Is your wife a member of the Parent-Teacher Association?"

Nor is it necessary to make our inventory of contacts by inquisitive or even formal methods. If through us a visitor is available, who can talk acceptably on any subject within our defined scope of "civic interest," we can ask him if any group of which he is a member might wish to hear him. If a member of our management, sales, or research staff has real information on an interesting topic, and can convey it acceptably, we can seek out a group which might want that information. In conversation with a staff member, a supervisor, or a group of department heads or foremen or supervisors, an honest but casual inquiry can be uttered which will bring the information we need. Perhaps we have mentioned a speaker, a product or service to be described, a picture or slide-film or lecture—any presentation which dramatically portrays any phase of our business, our products, our people, our customers: "If any of you think this might interest a group to which you belong, just let me know and I'll try to arrange for them to see (or hear) it." Valuable responses will come, some promptly, and some after surprising intervals. One will ask whether the speaker or picture can be available for his service club on the second Friday of next month. Another will report that he has been charged with providing the program for the South Side Improvement League next week, and could someone show them the picture? After an interval, another will come in to say that his wife would like to have the exhibit for her Red Cross Chapter next month.

These reports and inquiries, carefully recorded, are the beginning of our inventory of contacts with civic groups. The systematic recording of them is a valuable step in our program. The inventory can be tactfully enlarged by securing the printed lists of members or officers issued by many organizations and recording the names of those who are part of our organization or friends of our enterprise.

Another constructive step is the cultivation of contacts with leaders of such civic groups. The new presidents of the service clubs may be invited to visit the plant. Interesting publications may be offered to school superintendents. Efforts may properly be made to become acquainted with the neighborhood clergy. In a dozen ways our inventory of contacts will be listed and expanded, in a surprisingly short time.

The reader may correctly observe that this is public relations, not employee relations, a program for sharing information with the public, not with employees. Of course it is. But no program for sharing information with employees can overlook or omit these civic groups—or any organized part of the public. There are few methods which are better at stimulating our employees to receive, actually to seek, the information we want to share with them.

But, as with almost every medium, the final effective channel for sharing the information with employees is the channel of the line supervisor or foreman or straw boss. If he is not prepared as to attitude and equipped with knowledge, we can create both waste and damage by stimulating employee interest.

XVIII

EMPLOYEE MASS MEETINGS

The idea of a mass meeting of employees is attractive. At first glance it seems an almost perfect way to convey information to employees: It presents an opportunity to give the same information to the entire group at the same time. We feel that the same information offered in a form letter, house organ, or posted bulletin may not always be read or understood. We assume that because employees are present in body at the mass meeting they are present also in mind, and that the statements made in their hearing are heard and accepted. We value the effect of the living personality of the speaker as something which the printed word can seldom carry.

True, the mass meeting has advantages not found in other methods of sharing information. But it has some of the handicaps common to other methods, and it also has certain unique handicaps of its own.

Before we give to employee mass meetings a full and regular place in our program of sharing information with employees, we must survey this implement from several viewpoints. Our appraisal must deal with time, place, and organization, with subject matter and its manner of presentation, with the results desired and results to be avoided, and with the relative effectiveness of other methods of presenting or sharing our information.

The question of time concerns both long-range and short-range measures. In the long view, mass meetings are clearly not in order when they must be forced or held without clearly sufficient reason, when there is an atmosphere of conflict or distrust, or when employees are receiving adverse or false information from abler speakers or from unscrupulous enemies of the enterprise at other mass meetings. Constructive efforts to convey information to a mass group can seldom compete with these adverse conditions.

We have all heard and read of the frank and fearless employer in time of threatened conflict who called his "boys" together, told them the true facts, and spiked the guns of the "agitators" and trouble makers. It can be done, sometimes. Usually it cannot. And if the facts, plus the personality of the employer-speaker, are such that it can be done, almost surely there is no need to do it—the relation of mutual understanding is probably already there.

In terms of short-time measurement we face such troublesome questions of detail as these: What time of day? For how long? During working hours, or outside working hours? On company time, with attendance compulsory? On employee time, with attendance optional? At regular intervals? Once a week, once a month, or once a quarter? Irregularly, on special occasions? In what relation to other days or events? These questions are typical of many which come under the main question "when?" The answers, of course, depend on local and immediate conditions. But some of them are important in reaching constructive results.

For instance, the presentation of information to employees who have been required to attend the meeting must be more skillful than to those who have come at their own option. In the first case, we have a certain degree of automatic resistance, of preparation to refuse to believe. Therefore the information must be accurate, important, and understandable, and it must be dramatically and convincingly presented. In the second case, most of those who come voluntarily are prepared to receive the information but those to whom we are most anxious to give it do not attend!

The question whether attendance is compulsory or optional has deeper significance. We must assume that compulsory attendance is paid for by the employer. This is not only good sense but is practically unavoidable in any employment subject to the Fair Labor Standards Act. If held outside regular working hours such a meeting is likely to require payment at overtime rates for compulsory attendance. Whether paid for at straight time or overtime, the gathering becomes expensive and employees know it. This fact puts the meeting to a severe test. If the subject matter is worth while, and its presentation well planned, it may be desirable to emphasize the importance of it by paying this cost. If the subject is unimportant *in the mind of the employee,* either by its nature or by reason of its poor presentation, he loses respect for a management which wastes that much paid time of several hundred employees.

Such a meeting held outside working hours, whether on company time or employee time, has another requirement to meet. Purely from his own private standpoint, the employee must feel that the meeting is worth while *to him.* Whether he is paid for attending or is not paid, the message must be such as will give him a feeling that his private free time has not been needlessly invaded. He may even apply a harder test of value to a meeting outside working hours for which he is paid at overtime rates than he would to a similar meeting during working hours for which he is paid only straight time.

The employee mass meeting faces other problems in its relation to other days or events. Obviously it must not conflict with a baseball game, a union meeting, or a large number of planned fishing trips. But the relative timing must be planned even more carefully than merely to avoid conflicts. It must be timed in relation to what else has just happened or is scheduled soon to happen. It is difficult to hold such a meeting, no matter what the subject or who the speaker, in the heat of an election campaign without facing the unnecessary obstacle of suspicion of political motive. It is difficult to hold it soon after a propaganda attack on the employer or the industry without seeming to be on the defensive.

Finally, on the question of time, there must be a firm rule—"not too often." Emphasis can be given to a subject by the use of the mass meeting as a rare occasion. The loss of emphasis on any subject by making the mass meeting a habit is obvious.

After we hurdle the questions of time and timing we face similar questions of place. Under the broad question of place, we naturally think of mass meetings only where there is a mass to meet, that is, where there is a large number of employees. To agree on terms, we should need to set an arbitrary figure to identify a large number of employees. To some of us a hundred is a large number, large enough to constitute a mass meeting; to others the figure might be ten thousand. Perhaps we can more easily agree to talk about any number so large that the people in it can be most easily reached in a mass gathering.

Then the narrow or detail questions as to place. Have we an auditorium at the plant? Are we to go downtown for a meeting place? Shall we meet in the shipping room or the cafeteria? Can we have seats for everybody, or will all have to stand? Is there a suitable platform? Can everybody see the speaker? Can they all hear him directly, or must we have a loud-speaker?

As to organization, or the "how" of the mass meeting: Is there a chairman, or does the speaker just start? Is the attendance to be checked, and if so, how? Are questions to be permitted?

These and all the other questions of when, where, and how seem to be petty details. Most of them are. But they face us, they annoy us, they require answers in advance. Without listing and answering them, we cannot even begin our appraisal of the cost and value of the employee mass meeting. The questions mentioned here are merely examples; any employer considering the problem will have many other such questions, more specific, which he will be wise to weigh in advance.

Passing these, we meet the larger question of the purpose of the mass meeting. We are thinking of the general purpose of sharing information with employees. What information are we dealing with in this particular meeting? Is it a single, detached subject, or one of an integrated group of subjects to be covered in several such meetings? Two or three examples may serve to point out desirable uses of the mass-meeting technique.

A large corporation had just adopted the policy of furnishing to employees the printed annual report to stockholders. Each branch manager notified his respective employees that he would be glad to meet with those who so desired, at a given time, to discuss the report and answer questions about it. The attendance in most branches was more than 70 per cent of the total number of employees. Each manager had prepared himself as fully as possible to meet probable questions. In most cases questions were freely asked. These included some which the manager could not answer. He capitalized this opportunity by promising that the answer would be obtained from the technical officer at headquarters; then followed through on each such question and supplied the information later to the inquirer.

Such meetings were obviously timely. The attendance showed that the subject was rated important by most employees. The discussion and questioning improved the understanding of the information supplied in the report. Some of the questions led to better presentations in subsequent reports. Perhaps most important of all, the meeting dramatized the fact that the employees could find out what they wanted to know.

In another establishment, the first application of social security taxes was the occasion of a similar meeting. The establishment was located in a state which imposed an unemployment tax on employees as well as employers. The management took the opportunity to explain the coming deductions from the pay of employees. Clear presentation was made of the prospective benefits, in both old-age pensions and unemployment compensation. Steps required of employees to protect and secure their rights were mentioned. The willingness of the personnel office to assist employees in keeping their records, securing information, and later filing claims, was stressed. Of course the impressive amount of the Social Security taxes being paid by the company was mentioned.

Such instances portray elements of subject matter which are essential to mass meetings. The subjects were such that they obviously concerned the personal interests of all of the employees. They were directly connected with their jobs. They were subjects on which employees recognized the propriety of discussion by the employer. They were timely subjects. These tests are probably always applicable to subject matter for use in mass meetings.

The range of subject matter which meets these tests is still very broad—from wage rates to foreign wars and their effect on continuity of operation and employment. And the particular subject has a bearing on the selection of the speaker. If it is such a subject as either of those illustrated above, it is clearly desirable that it be handled by a local executive known to the employees. It might, however, be well handled by a specially equipped executive from outside the plant. Other subjects would clearly call for a speaker from outside the establishment—the president or treasurer from headquarters, a sales executive just returned from the Orient or from the Dust Bowl, or an advertising executive familiar with a new product or a new campaign.

No matter how well he knows his subject, such a man must meet other requirements or he should not be allowed to meet our employees. The personality of the speaker must be such as to impress employees favorably. His position should be one which they respect, and his manner must confirm that respect. He must convey information, not inspiration. (Employees, like the Greeks, have a word for the obviously inspirational type of speech.) Whether his message is good news or bad is less important than his attitude toward it and toward the employees, which should be serious, sincere, and frank. Frequently the result is more important in revealing the personality of the speaker, which becomes part of the personality of the company, than in conveying the immediate information.

A question which is almost peculiar to the mass meeting is important. Can this visiting executive do his job in such a meeting without overshadowing the line supervisors? Can he leave the impression that the foreman, the immediate work supervisor, the local superintendent and manager, are still the company, in the daily lives of employees? If he does a superlative job of conveying his information, revealing his own personality and ability, overshadowing and unconsciously belittling the local line management, the whole enterprise would be better off if he had stayed away and deprived us of both his information and his greatness.

One further test must be applied to the mass meeting as a medium for sharing information with employees: Is it the best available medium for the particular information, at the time, and in view of all circumstances? Unless it is measurably better than any other available medium, the weight of experience and comment indicates that preference should be given to some other available medium. There may be a few subjects and occasions which seem to suggest the mass meeting as clearly the best available medium. There are many more which can be better handled through the house organ, the bulletin board, or direct mail.

And, like every other medium, the success of the mass meeting is measured by the questions which it generates; and these questions surely lead us again to the line supervisor.

XIX

EMPLOYEE GROUP MEETINGS

In contrast to what we have described as the mass meeting, a succession of natural, almost casual, group meetings are taking place in every business or industrial establishment as part of the ordinary proceedings. Some of these meetings are the intentional channel for sharing some kind of information with employees, while others seem unrelated to this purpose. The fact is that all such meetings are essentially and inevitably contributing to the function of sharing information.

Therefore the inclusion of group meetings as one of the media for sharing information with employees is not an offering of any original thought. However, the pooled experiences in getting from such occasions a special value of this kind may lead us to a realization that we have scarcely touched the possibilities. One significant result obtained in one establishment and a different result in each of a dozen other places may suggest to us the possibility of a deliberate plan for using every group gathering to the best advantage in this process of creating understanding.

Before considering the actual types of groups which are continually meeting, it may be in order to agree, in our thinking, on some of the characteristics of group meetings in the sense in which we here use the term. It may not be possible to define them so exactly that we can always distinguish in one direction between a group meeting and a mass meeting, or in the other direction between a group meeting and a mere conversation. But certain descriptions are generally acceptable and necessary for this discussion.

For our purpose, the group meeting must be small. The exact limits of its size cannot be set. It must be small enough to permit free discussion, small enough to be the means of two-way conversation, instead of the usual process of speaker and listeners which characterizes the mass meeting. This element of two-way discussion is found in group meetings of varying size, but as a rule is most natural and effective when the group consists of a dozen or less. The desirable size compares with the "understanding unit" discussed in a later chapter.

A meeting of as many as fifty or sixty persons with a reasonable community of interest and similarity of status can sometimes be an effective channel for exchange of ideas and information. For instance, a periodical meeting of supervisors in a large organization, whether commercial or industrial, can evolve into a group meeting having the essentials we are now discussing. But that result is necessarily an evolution. So large a gathering tends to take on the characteristics of the mass meeting. All but five or six, probably all but one or two, of the number are likely to take the attitude of listeners. The degree of intimacy which will permit the effective impact of one personality or another is important. The best group meeting for our purpose is, therefore, one which is small enough for personalities to register.

Another characteristic of the group meeting which we are considering is that it should have a purpose, and a purpose bearing on the normal associations of the members of the group. Some typical purposes or functions of natural group meetings are viewed below. The thought offered here is that the accidental gathering of three or ten people who have some spare time after lunch does not constitute a "meeting" in this sense. If the same three or ten assemble in the same place, during the same spare time, for the purpose of discussing plans for an employee picnic or plans for protesting against the new summer schedule of hours, we have a group meeting. Given such a group meeting, some sharing of information can be accomplished. It is not even necessary that a management representative be present.

Next, a group meeting in our present meaning should be informal. It may have this characteristic in spite of the previously indicated need of a purpose. Informality in the conduct of the meeting has no necessary relation to accidental assembling of the group. Assembled for a known purpose, a dozen people need not adopt *Robert's Rules of Order* to accomplish the discussion of the subject before them. Informality promotes the two-way exchange we are seeking.

A meeting of a very small group may be rigidly formal and that of a larger group quite informal. But informality is to be expected and welcomed more naturally in the smaller group. Too much informality in a meeting of fifty or more is likely to promote disorder.

We are now looking at the group meeting as one which is small without exact number limits, one which has a purpose related to the normal associations of the group members, and one which is conducted in an informal but orderly manner. What meetings of this kind occur naturally in the life of the usual plant or establishment? Of course we can confine our question to companies or employing units where there is approval of employee expression and an actual desire for the understanding which is our objective. In the other type of employing unit we shall not find the group meetings for which we are looking. If some employers could find such meetings, they might succeed in discouraging them as dangerous to efficiency or discipline! So we shall select our examples in establishments where both employees and managers are free people and where understanding is as important as authority.

The ideal example in an industrial plant is probably the meeting of a committee to deal with plant safety or accident prevention. Almost universal experience has shown that safety itself is a product of understanding more than of engineering, a matter of mental attitude more than of physical safeguards alone. It follows that a committee on safety, which may include supervisors or foremen, will generally include a larger number of workers. Usually there will be included a technical-staff man known as the safety engineer or safety supervisor. Thus we have a desirable mixture of management and worker representatives engaged in a function which emphasizes common interest and minimizes the likelihood of conflicting interest.

The process of trial and error has brought most successful safety committees within our description of "small." Where a plant is so large that the representation of all departments would require a safety committee of forty or more, experience usually leads to the creation of more than one committee, usually by grouping departments, or even by setting up departmental committees for very large departments.

Informality is usual in the conduct of meetings of the safety committees. In many plants where smoking is generally prohibited, the safety meeting is held in a room where the members may smoke. Such meetings usually include a majority of workers in working clothes, reporting directly from the normal assignment at bench or machine or shipping scales. But informality does not degenerate into disorder, since there is usually a program for the discussion—a review of accidents since the last meeting, some discussion of accident statistics and costs, or consideration of safety suggestions which have been received.

It is difficult to conceive of a group meeting which can more completely exemplify this channel for sharing information with employees or one which will furnish a better model. Given this ideal medium, how can it be enlisted in the larger program of sharing information with employees, toward the major objective of understanding?

First we must recognize that gratifying progress has already been made in any plant where a safety committee exists and functions as described above. Management has recognized that employees have a dominant interest in safety, and has demonstrated this recognition. Both workers and management have found one field in which the common or mutual interest is clear. Both have found a way to pool their efforts toward the common objective. The process has necessarily involved the complete sharing of information, on the subject with which they are dealing. Before the days of workmen's compensation, and even since, it was not unusual to see an effort on the part of management to conceal, as far as possible, the facts about accidents in the plant. It was sometimes believed that the causes, conditions, and even the occurrence, of accidents to workers, could and should be concealed from other workers. The progress in the past twenty years has been spectacular.

The necessary agenda of such a safety committee meeting include subject matter which actually invites the introduction of collateral information. The presence of one or more management representatives provides the means for supplying the information. The responsibility and status of the employee members assures a further conveying of the information.

Let us attend a meeting of this committee. Only one accident has occurred since the last meeting, but that one was rather severe. Herman Heinz in the shipping department had his foot crushed. He will recover, but will be off work for two months. His compensation will amount to $60 a month, which will fairly well carry him through, since he has his home paid for. The safety supervisor or some other member can use this opportunity to comment on the large number of "our men who do own their homes." Or it may be mentioned that Herman has worked for the company for thirteen years and never had a lost-time accident before. This suggests that an up-to-date report be prepared for the next meeting on the relative frequency of accidents among older and newer employees. When the report comes in, it naturally shows the total number of present employees who have worked less than five years, five to ten, ten to fifteen, and so on.

Then the discussion of that report can lead to a question

about the ages of employees who have suffered accidents in the last year or two. When that report comes in, it necessarily shows how many of the total number of employees are over forty, over fifty, and over sixty. By the sharing of this information a counter-wave has been launched against the unfair and unfortunate propaganda that it is the custom of industry to "fire at forty."

Perhaps an installation is planned, or has been made, at a cost of $5,000, as the result of a recommendation of the committee to eliminate a possible hazard. Such an occasion invites an explanation of why the particular item cannot be charged to expense but must be treated as capital expenditure, how this means that the money must in effect be taken out of the profits which remain *after taxes* have been paid, and how it was therefore necessary to earn $8,000 or $12,000 or $15,000 in profits *before taxes* in order to provide the $5,000.

The committee may be considering the case of an employee who has been guilty of a violation of the safety rules, and advising with the management representatives on the discipline to be imposed. This gives an opportunity for unfolding the theory of discipline in general. It opens the way to identify the interest of employee and employer, jointly, in sustaining the orderly conduct of the enterprise. The consequence can be an exploration of many basic phases of the employee-relations policy of the company.

These and scores of other types of information can be shared naturally, almost casually, with a group meeting assembled to discuss plant safety. None of them needs to be "dragged in by the heels." An extraneous subject introduced without logical connection will blockade this channel, possibly forever.

The frank and intelligent sharing of information with and through a workmen's safety committee is only one example of the use of the group meeting to build understanding in this way. It is admittedly the best and most obvious example of a group meeting which is always available. It is a form which is not likely to be present in the organization of a store or an office. But there are countless opportunities to use other group meetings already existing, and to anticipate still others, as channels for sharing information with employees, in any kind of business or industrial enterprise.

In almost every plant or establishment there are, or should be, committees of employees to deal with problems created by the war or defense activities. Intensified guarding against fire or sabotage, identification of employees, time off for civilian defense duties, campaigns for sales of defense bonds —each of these is a pressing invitation for the active co-operation of an employee committee. Meetings to plan and carry out this co-operation can hardly be held without creating not merely opportunity but necessity for casual sharing of information on a dozen related subjects.

In establishments where employees have organized credit unions—and their number is growing rapidly—it is common practice for either the credit committee or the supervisory committee to solicit the advisory service of a management representative. While such a person should rarely be permitted to serve as an officer of an employee credit union, his help as an adviser can seldom be wisely withheld. The problems which such committees discuss are essentially parallel to those of a corporation. They include the accumulation of capital, its employment and protection, the selection of investment risks, the control of expenses and costs, the provision of reserves, and the adoption of intelligent dividend policies.

Could a better opportunity be provided to share information about the similar problems of the employer? It is for the benefit of his experience in just such problems that the treasurer, controller, or chief accountant is sought as adviser by the credit-union committees. With just a little foresight, and an attitude of willingness to share information, such an adviser can soon make it possible for the committee members to realize, and to pass on to their constituents, that the average corporation is a magnified credit union in which a thousand or a hundred thousand people have pooled their savings—a co-operative enterprise through which they expect their savings, or capital, to be employed, protected, and permitted to earn rents or dividends.

Mention should be made of employee committees which meet to plan or manage athletic teams, or picnics, or banquets, to administer apprentice programs, or to lay out vacation schedules. But we take the liberty of leaving the listing of such possibilities to the reader, and to present one suggestion which may appear radical at first glance. Where employees have formed or joined a union, the contact of management with any committee representing that union is second only to contact with the safety committee as an opportunity for sharing information with employees through group meetings. Such a meeting conforms to all the standards we have accepted as desirable for this medium. It carries a unique element of being naturally at the heart of the very function in which we are engaged. For whether the members of such a committee realize it or not, they are in fact charged with the duty of increasing understanding.

The fact that such committees frequently or usually come to the management with complaints has some advantages. The presentation of requests for adjustment of complaints demands the delivery of frank information. The explanation of complaints and grievances gives to management the much-desired knowledge of what the employees are thinking, what they want to know, what they do not understand.

We conclude the discussion of group meetings by reference to something which, in time and importance, comes far ahead of the meetings themselves. This is the earnest, arduous, thorough planning to make the best possible use of every such opportunity. In an establishment with a thousand or more employees, some one person in the upper levels of management can well devote the major part of his interest and time to this task. It involves knowledge of all the group meetings which occur regularly, and also those which are planned for special purposes. It may include arranging or suggesting some for which no other plans have been made. It requires study and arrangement for the selection of the person who is to carry the information.

A heavy part of the task is that of securing appropriate information from the sales, accounting, laboratory, engineering, purchasing, and other departments, the translation of these facts into form and language suitable for the particular group, and hours of consultation with the management representatives who are to be ready when the group meeting seems to call for the information.

Above all, the task requires planning for the continuity of the program, for a properly timed "follow-up" of each release of information through a group meeting. With such planned continuity, unlike many other media, the group meeting becomes a permanent and increasingly valuable channel. It is always a medium which functions most directly in the transformation of facts into understanding. The group meeting is in itself both a proof of some degree of understanding and an agency created to promote understanding and agreement for concerted action in its particular field. This field may be safety, recreation, or grievances; the process is equally one of exchanging information, reaching understanding, and doing something about it.

XX

THE GRAPEVINE

The grapevine is one of our oldest systems of communication. Its history, like its messages, is unwritten, but dates back almost to the invention of language.

It has features different from those of any other medium by which information is carried. It has never been seen, but its efficiency is known wherever human beings live or work or play together. Against barriers of walls, darkness, prohibitions, censorship, it actually gains potency. It seems actually to thrive under restraint or attempted suppression. It is at its best when its messages must "go around" someone for whom they are not intended.

As truly as it cannot be suppressed, so also it cannot be controlled in any positive way. Its facilities cannot be reserved for messages of a particular type or from a specified source. It cannot be "started" or used for the delivery of messages on scheduled time or to designated listeners.

It is unpredictable as to exact results. Like its natural namesake, it twists and turns, sending out branches in unexpected directions. A given fact, statement, or message, caught by a tendril of the grapevine, carried over its twisting, twining course, may become a strangely different thing at the successive points of its reception.

The grapevine has a reputation for mischief. In our thinking it has become associated with certain of the uses to which it has been put. We shrink and shudder at the sneaky, slimy idea of the "whispering campaign," the unpardonable, vicious use of the grapevine to exploit the credulity of all of us and thus blight the name of another.

The grapevine is as untraceable as it is unpredictable.

There is as little probability of learning where the story started as there is of mapping its course in advance.

In spite of its being invisible, intangible, uncontrollable, unpredictable, the grapevine is sometimes incredibly rapid. Many a man has had the experience of walking a few hundred feet from a room where an important decision had just been reached and being questioned by an acquaintance who had just learned of the decision from "another fellow," who of course had not been present in the decision room.

The grapevine grows best in what we may describe by the general name of institutions, that is, places or groupings where many people are together. These may be institutions in the usual sense of the word—dormitories, hospitals, prisons, boarding schools. They may be the type of grouping which brings the same people, or most of the same people, into contact daily or periodically—churches, day schools, clubs, stores, offices, factories.

There is no need to prove that the grapevine exists in stores, offices, and factories, the places where men and women are grouped together at work. Because it is there, because we have all been conscious of its effectiveness, we cannot leave it out of the discussion on sharing information with employees. We must recognize it as an agency by which information is always being carried to employees, whether we desire it or not. In fact, by the very nature of the grapevine, information which some authority hopes to conceal is likely to travel the faster.

We know that our buildings are equipped with lights, water, power, heat, and ventilation. Just as really, we must admit that they are equipped with grapevines. And so, realistically, let us appraise the grapevine in the program of sharing information with employees. Is it an obstacle? Is it a positive enemy of understanding between employers and employees? Or can it be enlisted? Be prepared for an answer of "yes" to all three questions.

The grapevine is an obstacle in the way of an employer who is ready to share information with employees. It has first call on the "receiving" facilities; the mental radio is forever tuned in on the grapevine wave-length, "standing by" for every program which comes over it. The grapevine is an obstacle to even getting a hearing from employees in the first steps of sharing information with them. If the tradition has been that the boss told them nothing but the grapevine brought the news, it will be hard to induce employees even to listen to information coming over another channel, especially one controlled by the boss.

It is an obstacle to having the proffered information accepted at face value, believed, understood. Even if information is received by the employee mind, the grapevine will carry criticism, interpretation, or hints of selfish motives behind the giving of the information.

To the rank and file in any institutional group, the grapevine is peculiarly a possession. It has been the secret and sacred property of the group, untainted by the influence of the boss, capable of tapping his store of hidden facts, capable of circumventing his censorship. And so in an entirely natural sense the grapevine is "ours." The bulletin board, information letter, house organ, and other new "stunts" belong to the boss. They are rivals of the ancient and trusted grapevine.

The grapevine is a positive enemy of understanding between employers and employees. Its very nature makes it a ready channel for the injection of discord and distrust, conceived in the world outside. The technique of mental sabotage does not require a conscious "fifth columnist" in the employee group. A sincere and friendly employee, repeating what seems to be a chance remark overheard in the beer parlor, is the ideal agent to start a message of suspicion down the mysterious course of the grapevine.

We cannot be realistic about the time and place in which we live, if we do not admit the existence of influences desiring the creation and stimulation of class hatreds. They cultivate the seeds of misunderstanding. They are inimical to industrial peace.

These influences are not the leaders of organized labor. Their plans and hopes are not the plans and hopes of any real trade or labor union. When their subversive doctrines are voiced by honest labor unionists, it is because their plausible insinuations have taken root in minds where their real purposes would be condemned and rejected.

These influences are the enemies of the real trade or labor union, definitely as they are the enemies of the other party to the collective bargaining process. In the lands where their ideals have ripened into dictatorships, suppression of every element of labor unionism has been both a result and a means toward a result.

Fanatical in the furtherance of a new order, they are unscrupulous, capable, and skillful. They use the grapevine to poison the minds of workers in their unions as readily as at their work. They make of the grapevine a positive influence against understanding and co-operation.

Can the grapevine be enlisted in the program of sharing information with employees? Can it be a builder of understanding, a channel for carrying messages which will create confidence instead of distrust? Emphatically, yes; it not only can be enlisted, but it will enlist itself automatically if the conditions are right.

Most messages for the grapevine are not deliberately initiated by anyone; they are usually self-starting. Although such messages include reports of facts or supposed facts, they are frequently comments on or interpretations of facts otherwise reported. The bulletin board asks for a special effort to prevent accidents; the grapevine explains that the superintendent has been "put on the pan" by the state inspector. A new man appears in a choice job in the laboratory staff; the grapevine explains that he is the new son-in-law of the chairman of the board. The manager leaves by plane for another state; the grapevine interprets the known facts to mean that he has gone to the Jones Company to hire a man to take the place of the master mechanic who has been slipping.

It is useless to try to send direct and accurate information from the employer to the employee over the grapevine. But the characteristics described in the foregoing paragraph, and earlier paragraphs, suggest the conditions needed to enlist the grapevine in a constructive way.

We have noted that the grapevine is invisible, uncontrollable, in most ways unpredictable, untraceable, secretive, persistent. We have said that it usually enjoys the confidence of the group it reaches. And, finally, we see that it carries supplemental and interpretative information rather than primary facts.

The most important fact of all is that the grapevine cannot successfully carry a message which does not fit the pattern of daily life in the group. Whether the whispered "tip" has originated in the planted comment of an outside agitator or in the spontaneous judgment of a member of the group, it will not be carried and believed unless it *can* be true in the light of existing attitudes and practices.

Let us re-examine the imaginary comments reported above; could they travel over the grapevine unless they had at least plausible validity, what your literature teacher called verisimilitude?

"The bulletin board asks for a special effort to prevent accidents; the grapevine explains that the superintendent has been put on the pan by the state inspector."

This message can travel successfully over the grapevine if these conditions are known to exist: (1) the accident experience has been bad; (2) the physical hazards have not been adequately guarded; (3) the employees have not been enlisted in the safety program; (4) suggestions, protests, and warnings from employees about unsafe conditions have been ignored; (5) the general attitude of management toward safety has been one of disregard, or one of formal and technical compliance with legal regulations.

This interpretation cannot get past the second relay on the grapevine if the following conditions exist: (1) the accident experience has been good, or has been improving; (2) every known physical hazard has been safeguarded as soon as discovered; (3) employees have been enlisted in the organized safety program; real representatives of groups of employees have served on permanent safety committees, with complete freedom of speech and action, and with complete, direct information about every accident; (4) suggestions and criticisms from employees, on the safety committee or off, have been welcomed by management and particularly by foremen, and have been acted upon promptly; (5) foremen and subforemen have reflected a management attitude which puts safety ahead of production, quality, or cost.

"A new man appears in a choice job in the laboratory staff; the grapevine explains that he is the new son-in-law of the chairman of the board."

This rumor can travel, be believed and repeated, and do damage to morale, if these conditions set the stage: (1) relatives of company officers have been getting good jobs in the plant; (2) promotions are customarily not made from within the ranks, or are made on the basis of favoritism; (3) employees or their representatives have not been either consulted or advised about the selection, retention, or promotion of personnel.

Such a report either would "fizzle" or would be received with a merely casual interest, harmless to morale, if the surrounding and preceding conditions were these: (1) relatives of influential officers have never enjoyed any preference in getting jobs; those who were hired had to "start from scratch" and progress on their merits; (2) employees, regardless who they are, have been hired, retained, and promoted with first regard to ability and with due regard to seniority; (3) methods of selection, rating, and promotion have been adequately explained to employees or their representatives, not by way of issuing edicts, but rather by way of seeking understanding and advice; (4) methods of personnel administration and general policies have been consistent, and have been observed in spirit, not only in hiring and promotions but in discipline and discharges.

And so we might continue to argue the case that the grapevine, besides being an influence on employee attitudes, is even more largely an expression of those attitudes. It cannot carry rumors or insinuations which do not fit the real picture.

How can it be enlisted in a constructive program of sharing information with employees?

The relationship between the employees and management must be basically right. Policies must be sound, and consistently followed.

The established attitude of management must be one of frankness. If any desired information can be correctly obtained by employees by asking, the grapevine cannot "sell" clandestine or *sub rosa* rumors. It can and will carry explanations and interpretations of true facts. Particular attention can be paid to cultivating and satisfying the curiosity or interest of employees who are looked upon by their fellows as capable leaders, reliable bearers of news, and as competent interpreters of its meaning.

Finally, in this as in every other successful method of sharing information with employees, the sharing must take place at the point of closest and most frequent contact—the immediate supervisor. As always, the foreman or supervisor must have built up a relationship which will permit an employee to ask *him* about the safety program or the new laboratory man. The foreman or supervisor must be ready and prompt to answer questions which are proper, and patiently willing to explain why, if other questions cannot be immediately answered.

Top management cannot put information on the grapevine. The immediate supervisor can. Therefore, to use the grapevine constructively, top management's task is to equip the foreman in advance, as fully as possible, with what he needs to know when questions come to him, and to guide him, by example, to a healthy attitude of welcoming questions, and answering them with frankness.

XXI

WHAT ABOUT THE UNIONS?

No one can deny that the problem of sharing information with employees is different in an establishment which is unionized and in one which is not. But the nature of the differences is not immediately clear. The differences need to be explored, weighed, and catalogued. They are not barriers to an honest program of understanding. Rather they are guides to the way the program must be planned.

A strange thought to many employers will be this: In general, it is easier to share information effectively with unionized employees than with those who are not unionized. An understanding of this premise, even without full acceptance of it, is essential to a full understanding of the purpose behind the whole plan we are considering.

To distinguish between the problems in the two types of establishments, we must discuss mainly the resistance factors, the obstacles to sharing information. Some of them, of course, are basic human characteristics. Since union and nonunion employees are equally human, these basic psychological difficulties are common in our relations with both groups.

Under other chapters we have discussed some of the problems which are basic in sharing information with employees. For instance, we have considered the lack of interest because our information does not seem to fit the vital concern of the employee, the instinctive suspicion of employer motive, and the danger of misinterpretation of complicated information. While any of these difficulties may be intensified under union conditions, or at least in certain stages of union relationships, they are all present under nonunion conditions also.

Our interest can profitably be centered on these difficulties in sharing information with employees which are peculiarly related to the question of whether the employees are organized or unorganized. One common error keeps many employers from seeing the constructive function of unions in the whole program of building better understanding with employees, in sharing information with them as well as in other ways. This is the error of considering the union as an entity separate and distinct from our employees. The consequence is the belief on our part that the union, coming from somewhere in outer space, is a wedge driven between us and our "boys."

It would be useless to deny that this "wedge" idea is often correct. But such conditions are not of the essence of labor organization. No matter how they arise, we can cure them by taking the position that the union *is* our employees as a group, organized in a certain way for certain purposes. If our employees as individuals become convinced that this is our honest attitude, they can be trusted to make it their attitude. Given reasonable time, any group of American workers, in possession of regular jobs, will *make* their union represent them. Employees who were unorganized last year and who this year have all joined one union, or seven different unions, have not changed their identities. The union or unions through which they deal with us are not entities in themselves. They *are* our employees.

One realistic attitude should help us to adjust our thinking on this point. We should accept the fact that, in most of our early relations with them, the union spokesmen believe—not always fancifully—that we as employers are intent on driving a wedge between them and their constituents, our employees.

How can it be easier to share information effectively with employees who are unionized than with those who are not? Some of the answers may seem to be theoretical. Seen merely as theories, they are capable of being tested. Experiments in actual tests have built a large enough body of experience to provide substantial, almost overwhelming, evidence in support of these theories.

The first purpose of unionization, always first in time and usually first in importance, is collective bargaining. The immediate labor objective in collective bargaining is usually the acquisition of advantages at the expense of the employer. The early amateur techniques of both parties in collective bargaining are horse trading, concealment of facts, and implied threat and counterthreat. These techniques usually continue until the employer realizes that the true objective of collective bargaining is understanding. When he demonstrates this realization, collective bargaining, with its implications of conflicting interest, gradually evolves into collective planning with the implications of mutual interest.

Collective planning demands more than mere acquiescence. It demands more than the semi-emotional "feeling" of understanding. It demands intelligent understanding, based on common knowledge of facts which affect the common interest of employee and employer.

Many of the well-established national unions carry this concept to the employer in their first approach. Several hundred union agreements now in effect begin with the following clause, drafted and presented by the union officials:

> The general purpose of this Agreement is, in the mutual interest of the employer and employee, to provide for the operation of the plant (or plants) hereinafter mentioned under methods which will further, to the fullest extent possible, the safety, welfare, and health of the employees, economy of operation, quality and quantity of output, cleanliness of plant and protection of property. It is recognized by this Agreement to be the duty of the Company and the employees to co-operate fully, individually, and collectively, for the advancement of said conditions.

Another international brotherhood, one of the strongest,

both in numbers and in bargaining effectiveness, uses this preamble:

> The Company and the Union have a common and sympathetic interest in the [blank] industry. Therefore, a working system and harmonious relations are necessary to improve the relationship between the Company, the Union, and the Public. All will benefit by continuous peace and by adjusting any differences by rational common-sense methods. Progress in industry demands a mutuality of confidence between the Company and the Union. To these ends this agreement is made.

Such agreements lay the constitutional foundations for a way of life in the industrial establishment. This way of life is the way of understanding. Such understanding is the fruit of knowledge. Without sharing information with his employees, an employer cannot expect their co-operation, individually or collectively, in the furtherance of their own safety, welfare, and health and the consequent reduction of his own costs of accidents and absenteeism. Without supplying them the information necessary, he cannot expect their intelligent co-operation toward economy of operation, quality and quantity of production, and so forth.

Therefore, the first theory to be tested is this: The logical long-time objective of unionization is co-operation based on understanding. This objective will be adopted most quickly if the employer makes available the information from which mutuality of interest can be recognized and the furtherance of mutual interest intelligently planned.

A second theory of advantage of union conditions in sharing information with employees is likewise supported by majority experience, although the unsuccessful minority of "tests" is large. The voluntary organization of employees into unions is at least partially an evidence of self-assertion. Self-assertion is usually an evidence of thinking. Without argument it must be admitted that not all joining of unions is voluntary. Also it must be admitted that some self-assertion is evidence of feeling rather than thinking. Those cases of forced unionization on the one hand and self-assertion based on emotional disturbance on the other hand are elements in the cases where the general theory is not supported.

But in the majority of cases, organization is voluntary; self-assertion is the result of thinking. If an employer will express this belief, in words and actions, he will usually find the union spokesmen agreeing with it. He will find them proud to show their ability as thinking leaders of thinking men. When this attitude has been achieved, there is a pressing need for information as the raw material for the thinking process.

A third premise is that the representative of organized employees, no matter how he was chosen, needs a constant supply of information to enable him to show his worthiness of the leadership trust imposed on him. We discuss this more fully under the subject of differences between "outside" and "inside" unions.

A fourth advantage of union conditions in the program of sharing information with employees is perhaps more important than all the others. This is the general difference in the attitude of employees toward information brought to them by their own union representatives. They are more ready to listen to these spokesmen than to the employer, except in the rare cases where they have already grasped the mutuality of interest. They are more ready to believe the information brought by their own spokesmen; they assume that these spokesmen have been able to test and verify the information before passing it on to their fellow employees. They have a sense of dignity and right to information thus obtained, rather than a suspicion that the employer is patronizing them with a gift of information.

This inclination to receive and believe the information brought by their own spokesmen does not close the minds of employees to information obtained through the natural channel of the management line. It can, in fact, greatly improve the reception of information so conveyed. If what the foreman says can be checked and found true or logical, by the standard of what the union representative says, the foreman becomes automatically a reliable source of information.

It may be disturbing to know that our management line needs the implied sponsorship or endorsement of the union representative in order to make it a dependable channel of information in the minds of employees. Disturbing or not, it is wise to accept this premise. Our objective is to share information with employees so as to build for understanding. If natural reactions make the verification by the union officer valuable, there is no reason why we should not rejoice that our management line can thereby be made a more effective instrument for our basic purpose.

One other advantage for the union condition frequently exists. That is the provision of a test of the effectiveness of the program of sharing information with employees. The union spokesman in most cases reflects to the employer the thinking of his employees. The employer can usually know, from the attitude of these spokesmen, whether the information supplied through them or any other channel has reached the minds of employees, been understood by them, and been made the basis of their reasoning and proposals.

There is some difference in the opportunity when the union is represented by an "outside" paid secretary or business agent, and when it is represented by a secretary, steward, or committee chosen from among the employees themselves. The important fact in either case is this: Basically, union representatives want information about the employer's business.

Most of us have the feeling that an "outside" union representative is unfamiliar with our business and its problems, that he will not understand the facts if he has them. Against this is the fact that he is likely to be much more experienced than any of our employees in the conduct of relations through a union, much wiser in grasping the significance of business information as applied to wages, hours, working conditions, and future prospects of employment. He is likely to be more positive, more confident, more courageous, in presenting and interpreting information to our employees, because they are not his only constituents.

The representative or committee chosen within the establishment is subject to more of the hazards of "pure" democracy. He or it must satisfy the single group of constituents, or lose the place of honor and leadership. The securing of information to pass on to fellow workers is an achievement, a credit to the representative or committeeman. His ability to interpret the information may be small at first. Such ability develops rapidly in most men so placed. The "inside" spokesman for the union employees needs either constant concessions or constant supplies of accurate information in order to maintain his leadership. He needs one or both, because he does not have the degree of independence, security, and authoritarian status possessed by the "outside" representative.

Any union representative dealing with an employer, either bargaining or adjusting grievances, is a living request for information. We have been painfully slow, almost all of us, in realizing the constructive possibilities of this fact. We have taken a defensive, secretive stand against what we considered the prying of such people into the business of management. We have seen examples of facts twisted to suit a program of agitation, facts half-told in order to create conflict between employer and employee. The more we have barred the sources of information to union representatives, the more dramatic and unfavorable has been their use of the fragments they did obtain; and the more persistent and circuitous have been their methods of obtaining what they could use.

Frankness toward the so-called labor politician helps him

to become a labor statesman. One of the "outside" union representatives told a large employer an amusing story—on himself! He had invested $100 of his own money in one share of preferred stock of the employer's corporation so that he could receive the annual report to stockholders, before he knew that the identical report was given to every employee for the asking! Like hundreds of similar union spokesmen, he has now turned his talents away from planning clever ways to obtain information, and toward the job of understanding, interpreting, and using constructively the information which is frankly furnished to him on request.

XXII

RESULT: QUESTIONS

Sharing information with employees is pictured here as a road toward understanding. The sharing may be done in many ways or through many implements. It may be a sharing of many kinds of information. No matter what the subject matter or the method, the results may vary widely.

In preceding chapters we have looked hastily at some of the subjects, kinds of information, at some of the methods or channels, and at problems of appropriate time and place. In all these views we may seem to have given small space to measuring the respective efficiencies of the methods. The reason is that the conveying of information has not been accepted or proposed as an object in itself. Rather it has been, in all our thinking, merely a means, merely one means, toward an end. The end, the compelling objective, is *understanding*.

Information can be conveyed in a manner which is effective but which at the same time creates irritation and antagonism, not because of the nature of the information, but because of the manner of its delivery. A method which patronizes or belittles the employee, which imputes to him a childish intelligence, which implies that he has been gullible enough to be misled by some misinformation, may inform him accurately but will not promote real understanding. A method which crudely suggests that there is a lot which the employee cannot comprehend unless he allows someone to explain it to him is not likely to induce him to ask anyone for any explanation. An approach which obviously offers limited facts as a bait to awaken curiosity is more likely to produce distrust and resentful silence than interest and constructive questions.

As a step toward understanding, the conventional media for sharing information with employees will be most successful if they (1) carry a conviction of sincere desire on the part of management to share correct information with employees and dispel the suspicion that there are funds of information hidden and guarded; (2) produce interest in more information either on the same subjects or others; (3) stimulate questions. Stated more briefly, any medium will do a valuable job if it stimulates confidence, interest, and, above all, questions.

The questions will be honest requests for facts, tricky efforts to pry, clever efforts to produce inconsistencies. No matter what may be the spirit in which the questions are asked, management will welcome them if it is convinced that sharing information is one road toward understanding. Questions bring the priceless chance to tell its story to employees.

In the summing up we shall find ourselves rejecting some methods of sharing information which seem efficient, accepting some which seem only partially efficient, and urging a laborious, tedious supplement to each method and all methods which have been discussed.

The supplement is laborious and tedious because it demands perpetual planning and daily doing. It requires the active enlistment and co-operation of a staggering number of people. It is essentially an "inside job" for which no expert or professional counsellor can be hired.

Without the supplement we may have a heavy program and ample machinery for sharing information with employees. Combining the test standards of efficiency and importance, our inventory might include the following, in the order of decreasing value—from "double plus" to "double minus": (1) the grapevine; (2) the annual report; (3) the house organ; (4) committees and groups (of employees); (5) civic groups; (6) direct mail; (7) films and slides; (8) bulletin boards; (9) mass meetings; (10) pay inserts.

At least ten other media can be suggested, some equal in value to some of those named above. Enough are in this inventory to permit the picture to take shape. Let us assume that all channels likely to prejudice our program have been shelved and all channels of the "plus" type have been used, wisely and successfully. What have we achieved? That is our logical query; but in a practical approach, it is easier to sum up the results we have not achieved, can never achieve, through these means alone.

We have not given the information which "was wanted." No matter how carefully we have selected the subjects and topics, much of what we have given has been information for which there was no desire. Such channels as small employee groups or committees have a correcting influence; two-way discussions are likely to reveal genuine interest in certain subjects. But in general our best-planned program for using all approved media will carry an abundance of surplus information, an incomplete coverage of desired information.

We have not produced knowledge of the kind which represents comprehension, knowledge of meaning as well as fact. The cumulative reception of factual information must in time produce an attitude, a reaction, which is in line with the facts. But the presentation of facts through all the best media available, even if fully received, does not produce knowledge of the kind we want to produce. An employee, or a stockholder, may receive and read and memorize the annual financial report, without comprehending the financial status or progress of the company.

The kind of knowledge we want our employees to possess requires more than the passive reception of facts. It requires the active reception of facts, the exploration of meanings and of the relation of fact to fact. It requires pursuit of additional facts to complete a picture the outlines of which are suggested by the given facts. It requires activity of the mind and expression of that activity. It requires the framing of questions and the opportunity to voice those questions. If our program of sharing information with employees, through all the channels and methods named above, is completely successful, the result—and the evidence of success—will be questions!

The supplement we must provide is an adequate plan for meeting these questions. Meeting them does not mean parrying them; it means answering them.

Some of these questions will be annoying or embarrassing. Some of them will drive us, the employers, into fields of thought which we have avoided. Some of them will test the completeness of our willingness to share information with employees; they will force us to ask ourselves if we have really meant it.

If there have been conscious or unconscious limitations in our willingness, we shall be in a most unfortunate position, much worse than if we had stayed with the narrow but consistent position that information about the business was none of the business of the employee.

The inevitable result of a good program of sharing information with employees is a crop of questions—requests for more information, or for explanations of given facts. The first of such questions which is met with evasion, subterfuge, or arbitrary refusal is the end of our progress toward understanding and confidence. We have created and verified the belief that we seek to convey certain facts which probably tend to create a favorable impression and to conceal other facts which would tend otherwise. We have in effect advertised that there are facts which, if known to our employees, would cause them to regard us with disapproval, suspicion, or dissatisfaction.

The employer who supplies to his employees only those facts and figures which portray him as benefactor, or as an object of sympathy, is likely to get no good result from the beginning. The employer who enters upon a program of frank sharing of information with employees and later admits that he meant it "within certain limits" has injured his relation with employees, probably seriously and permanently.

It is dangerous to enter upon the use of any of the conventional media for conveying information to employees until we have thought through the sequence. Is there any question which can be prompted by any of this volunteered information which we are unwilling to answer? If so, let us retire to, or remain in, the secretive silence of the days gone by.

The consequence of starting to share information with employees is interest, expressed in questions, or requests for more information. The supplement to the best media for conveying information is a thorough preparation to meet the resulting questions, fully, frankly, and gladly.

This preparation is first a matter of attitude, as indicated above. If we volunteer the information, perhaps in the annual report, that our total payments of wages and salaries were $2,000,000, and if one or more employees come in or write in to ask how much of that was the salary of the president, are we prepared to be willing to answer?

If there are doubts and reservations as to how far we are willing to go in answering all the questions employees may present, perhaps we should postpone the idea of building understanding by sharing information with employees. But there are definite relations between the subjects on which information is volunteered and the subjects on which questions will be asked.

There may be fields in which some employers are willing to share information and answer questions without reservation, other fields in which they are willing to share information of their own selection but unwilling to answer all conceivable questions. In such a case, any program of sharing information is so hazardous that its planning and execution require wisdom of a rare type.

For instance, consider the reference above to the question about the salary of the president. A management which is unwilling to answer that question will never start sharing information on the subject of salaries. But that same management may be anxious to place before employees the information that the wage cost of their product is high compared with that of a competitive product. That management may feel that they can safely supply information about wages without prompting questions about salaries.

They may prepare frank and accurate statements showing total wages paid, average wage rates and wage earnings per employee, wage costs in proportion to total costs and to total sales, and wage totals compared with last year or with 1929. They may be willing to answer any question which arises about the number of wage earners in the different years, about the production per wage earner, about the relative cost of living here and in the competitor's town, or the cost of living now and last year.

But can a safe fence be built around the questions to be asked? Perhaps this management pays wages to its foremen and includes that in wage costs, whereas the competitor pays salaries to its foremen. If any question or answer brings out this fact, the fence is breached; almost any question about salaries may follow.

Or some other management, willing to share information with employees, with reservations, may feel that the subject of taxes is a safe one. And through some appropriate channel they prepare to make the selected facts known to employees. In succession they discuss their total taxes of all kinds for the previous year and compare that total with earlier years. They translate total taxes into dollars per worker, percentage of sales, percentage of dividends. What questions may be anticipated? One employee may want to know about the assessed value of the industrial property, how the assessment compares with the real investment, and how that ratio compares with the ratio of assessment on his little home. Another employee may ask someone how much of the total was taxes on profits.

In that way he may learn about the profits, learn facts the management did not intend to discuss. He may raise questions about why it would not be better to pay higher wages, make less profit, and pay less taxes.

The examples of the way in which information about one subject may stimulate questions about other subjects can be multiplied indefinitely. The point is not that questions will arise which cannot be clearly answered by a management prepared to answer them. The point is that any management which sets out to use the process of sharing information with employees to build for better understanding is almost required to commit itself in advance to welcome and to answer almost any question, anticipated or not.

If there is a question asked which cannot be safely answered because the information might reach a competitor and be used to the detriment of this enterprise, that fact can be the answer. But such an answer demands the utmost skill and honesty.

Unless the questions are welcomed as the revelation of what the employee wants to know, the management has not reached full belief in this method of creating understanding. Understanding involves knowledge by the employer of what the employee wants to know, as well as a whole-hearted resolve to give him the information he wants. The end-point to be thus reached is the comprehension, by the employee, that he has a vital stake in the success of the enterprise, and that his stake is being protected by the way in which the enterprise is being managed. If the questions are asked and merely ignored or evaded, the road toward understanding is blocked. The seeds of skepticism, suspicion, and misunderstanding are nurtured.

And the best use of the best media for supplying information to employees will achieve the inevitable result of stimulating and inviting questions.

XXIII

THE LINE SUPERVISOR

When employees ask questions, who is going to answer them? When house organs, bulletin boards, speakers, annual reports, or personal letters have aroused the interest of an employee in any subject of concern to him, where is he to go for more facts, more explanation?

First, where is he likely to go, in the absence of any implied direction? If the letter or bulletin or article does not say to ask the personnel officer, or write to the treasurer, or phone to the information service, who is the person most likely to be consulted by the average employee? In most cases it will be someone to whom the employee can talk—does talk—naturally and often, and who at the same time is, in the mind of the employee, part of the management. In most cases, he will reveal his interest and direct his questions to his immediate work supervisor.

From this supervisor he normally receives his first instructions as a new employee—instructions about company and departmental rules and about working hours, the time clock, and working locations, and instructions about the work, its important points requiring accuracy or quality, and its proper quantity per hour, per day, or per week. From this same supervisor he receives daily advice as to correction of errors, observance of safeguards against accident, complaints of customers or inspectors, chances for improvement and promotion, and the prospects of work ahead. With this same supervisor he takes up the infinite variety of day-to-day problems about the work, about his pay, about his grievances, his seniority, his days off. From this same supervisor he has gathered most of his impressions and opinions about company policies and attitudes, about the personalities, abilities, and characters of the "higher ups."

In a natural and inevitable way, this supervisor is the company to this average employee. And so, in an equally natural course, he will take his new questions about the business to this same supervisor. Any management which uses one of the conventional media for employee information, and thereby generates questions, must take positive steps if it wishes to guide those questions to any point or person other than the immediate foreman or supervisor.

This can be done as suggested above. The article about the research project can say, in effect, that questions will be answered and additional information supplied by Mr. Jones, the director of the laboratory. The annual report can similarly guide inquirers to the treasurer or the office manager or the personnel officer. This will in many cases divert the questions from the foreman or work supervisor.

This will in many cases do more. It will say, between the lines: "Your foreman or supervisor is all right in his job, but his job is to get the work done, not to explain or even understand complicated problems of management. You should depend on him for instructions about the daily work; but, if you are really interested in this thing the company is doing, go to somebody higher up, who really knows."

Another plan can be followed quite successfully. Making no effort to direct questions to anyone other than the foreman, the foreman himself can be coached to pass the question and the questioner on to someone specially designated. This respects to a somewhat greater extent the natural line of contact and supervision, but it also implies the inability of the supervisor to handle information of the kind involved. Some complex subjects, some unforeseen questions, must be shunted in this way. But no management can have the kind of line supervisors it needs if it says to them, in effect: "We don't believe you are equipped to answer these questions. We don't trust you to explain such things to your men. We don't want you to try. Send them to the office."

Where the question must be referred to someone else, higher in the line, or in a technical position, the manner of doing so can make all the difference in the world; and the manner will be a direct reflection of the attitude of top management toward its line supervisors.

For instance, a supervisor or foreman has been asked a question he cannot answer. He can shunt the question in this way: "How would I know that? If you want to know, go ask Jones in the laboratory. That's his job."

If he does this, has he built for understanding? Has he made himself a better supervisor, a better producer of co-operation, a better representative of management? Hardly.

Or again for instance, he can say: "Well, Bill, you've got me. I never thought about that, and I don't know, and I'd like to know. Let's you and I go over to the laboratory and ask Jones; he can tell us."

If he does this, has he humiliated himself? Has he lost any of the respect of his fellow worker? Or has he moved a little closer to this worker by demonstrating a share in the interest which prompted the employee's question? In my opinion, this type of reply to a few questions is even better than being invariably ready with an immediate answer. But if foremen and supervisors are to handle questions, there must be a reasonable majority of cases in which they are prepared to answer readily and correctly. And if they are the right men in their jobs, they can do just this.

One corporation executive in an intimate conference rejected the idea of encouraging, or even permitting, foremen to answer employee questions about such things as company finances, for instance. Did he not want employees to ask questions and obtain information of this kind? Of course he did. But he explained that his corporation's capital structure, for one thing, was too complicated for a foreman to understand or to explain correctly: "I welcome such questions from employees," he said, "but I want them to bring their questions to me, not to some foreman."

Another member of the group asked him, "Can you explain this complex capital structure so that the employee can understand it?"

"Yes, of course," he answered.

"Then why can't you explain it so that the foreman can understand it?"

The corporation executive started to answer, then laughed. Six months later he was committed to a program of sharing information with employees through the channel of the regular line organization—even the complicated financial information.

It is not difficult to foresee bad results from implying to employees that their line supervisors are not competent to discuss this information with them. But there is a less evident danger in the practice of supplying such information directly to the employee from a source higher than the foreman himself. This is the danger of developing in the mind of the employee the consciousness that he knows or understands more about the company business than the foreman knows, that he has been considered intelligent enough to understand some complicated or confidential information which the foreman was unable to explain to him. This might build toward understanding between the employee and the treasurer, but not between the employee and the foreman.

The willingness to permit and encourage questions to be directed to the foreman or immediate supervisor has a by-product value which is highly important in the movement toward understanding. This is the growth of the supervisor himself.

Those who have been dealing with problems of employer-employee relations for even a few years have seen a great development of what was called "foreman training." They have also seen an effort to eliminate the connotation of teacher and classroom by putting the emphasis on the "conference method." Most recently they have seen—and encouraged—the development of conferences and conference material by foremen themselves, through a country-wide federation of foremen's organizations.

The inference that a foreman who has worked his way up to that job, who has been "handling men" for years, can be taught something or needs to learn something about his own job, is a handicap to any such program. The same handicap meets the effort of a management to convey company information to foremen. They instinctively feel that what they need is, not information or propaganda or instruction in methods of foremanship, but recognition, authority, and backing.

But if employees consistently come to a foreman with questions the foreman cannot answer, a powerful incentive has been created for the foreman to seek out information in which he has not previously been much interested. He is likely to make an effort to prepare himself for questions which may come from a story in the house organ, an address reported in the local newspaper, or a bulletin on the bulletin board. His self-respect is not affected by seeking information to give to his fellow workers; that is very different from being given information on the assumption that he needs it for himself.

This place of the line supervisor in the program of sharing information with employees compels consideration at an earlier stage in the program. The necessity of supporting the position of the foreman, as the effective link in the chain of work production, leads to realization that he must have an early and positive part in any conveying of information to employees.

If the house organ is to carry a story of the establishment of a South American branch, the foreman should know the substance of the story before the house-organ issue is in the hands of employees. If the bulletin board is about to carry a notice of two weeks' shutdown for general repairs, the foreman should be recognized by giving him advance information. If the general manager is planning a direct-mail letter to all employees, explaining the new working requirements resulting from the defense program, the foreman should know about it before some employee on the morning shift brings it to him with a question.

The foreman or immediate supervisor should know in advance, not only that certain information is about to be given to employees, not only the mere content of the letter or article or bulletin, but a substantial amount of explanatory and supplemental data to make him a respectable source of answers for questions employees may raise. A bulletin is necessarily brief, a direct-mail letter can be a little longer, a house-organ article considerably longer. But each of them leaves a larger or smaller body of related information which cannot be satisfactorily treated in print. It is this supplemental information, coupled with advance knowledge of the announcement, which will so greatly aid the foreman—aid him to grow in self-respect, confidence, and sense of responsibility.

But one more advantage is to be gained from full recognition of the place of the foreman in this picture. He should not only know in advance that a certain announcement is to be made and know its contents and all pertinent supplemental information; he should also be enlisted as an active factor in preparing, phrasing, and timing the announcement.

This suggestion may seem radical to many employers who have long followed a broad-gauge program of sharing information with employees. It is offered with full knowledge that even some of the most progressive employers have not used it, will not readily favor it. In the following chapter, some discussion relates to such enlistment of foremen in its effect on the foremen. The point here is its effect on the program of sharing information.

In the natural course, the foreman, the line supervisor, knows very clearly the reaction of employees to the last information supplied them, and to the manner of its communication. He learns whether the house organ or the recent direct-mail letter sent to the homes was resented when a bulletin-board notice would have been accepted.

He can advise not only as to the channel or medium to be used but as to the timing of the "release." If he knows there is some confusion following the first payday at the new rates, he may advise that time be allowed for clearing up all questions and misunderstandings on that before any new information is supplied.

In other circumstances he and his fellow supervisors may point out that a subject which really needs the full treatment possible in the house organ should not be delayed until the next issue. Rather, a brief immediate statement should be made on the bulletin board; the inferior medium for that particular item should be used because it is important that the information be given *now*.

Whether our business is building tractors or washing machines or children's toys, selling lumber or cloaks and suits or stationery, the immediate supervisor is the one who carries responsibility for direct leadership. Whether we call him foreman, lead man, straw boss, office manager, chief clerk, or section manager, his leadership is the deciding factor in the efficiency of our organization.

Because we rely so heavily upon him, no program for building understanding can succeed without him. No plan of sharing information with employees can flow past or around him without reducing his effectiveness as the driving gear in our business machine.

If the line supervisor cannot provide information when his fellow workers reflect the interest created through the comments of the dentist, and the wife who attended the club meeting, we have failed in our real purpose. We have been unprepared to share information with employees through the channel which normally brings them information about their work.

If the line supervisor is not prepared in his attitude and not prepared to welcome such questions and discussions, we have failed at a point farther back in our program.

And if we so fail, the penalty is not only the loss of an opportunity to bring knowledge and understanding to our employees. The real penalty is the humiliation of the supervisor, his moral demotion in the respect of his fellow workers, and his reduction in value and effectiveness as a work supervisor.

But the line does not end with the work supervisor or the straw boss. The line reaches to the last man who works. The leadership of the immediate supervisor is reflected in the knowledge, the understanding, the attitude of the men who work with him. These men, especially the older workers, are a part or extension of the supervisor himself in his function of conveying information.

A group of line supervisors, in a serious conference, were discussing the understanding and application of company policies in employee relations. The immediate question was where to put the burden: Who is the person in the organization who can best explain and demonstrate company policies, particularly to the new employee? Due weight was given to the function of the employment or personnel man and the safety supervisor, and other such staff men, in the instruction of the new employee before he goes on the job. However, the overwhelming majority agreed that the immediate line supervisor or foreman must be relied upon to do the job. As the discussion went around the group, one old, practical, hard-boiled foreman announced his disagreement. He expressed a fundamental and important truth in these words:

"It's the guy he works with. The new fellow is going to learn more about what you call the policy of the company and all that stuff from the old-timer that he works alongside of for the first few days than he is from all the brass hats in the place. And what he learns that first few days, you ain't going to be able to unlearn him very easy."

No medium for carrying information can duplicate or displace the supervisor who lives with employees in their daily work. No program of using conventional media for conveying information to employees can be wisely planned without the benefit of his advice. No information can be completely and intelligently shared with employees without his effective supplementary and explanatory work. No question raised by an employee can safely be diverted around him without weakening him in his essential function.

In sharing information, in building understanding, as in managing the daily work, there is no substitute for the line supervisor.

XXIV

BACK TO THE UNDERSTANDING UNIT

We have tried to high-light a picture of the days of simpler organization and smaller units in business and industry. The fact that such a unit did exist, that it was the usual establishment and not the exception, is history. The belief that the size of the unit was in itself an aid toward understanding is in line with history, but history which is a matter more of memory than of written record. This belief is in harmony with the conclusions to be reached by reason and logic and a working knowledge of human nature. Most convincing, perhaps, it is in accord with the experience of today where there has been an intelligent return to the fundamentals of the small unit or group as an area of understanding.

There is no turning back to the small unit as the pattern for organization of our industrial enterprise without abandoning the fruits of our achievement in mass organization and production. The breaking up of our industries, stores, and utilities into hundreds of thousands of small units means lowering our plane of living. It means the surrender of our national efficiency and our reduction in the scale of nations to a position of weakness, poverty, and subjection. But the restoration of the understanding unit *within* even the largest of our mass organizations can be accomplished. If it is done, the efficiency of our free-enterprise system will be increased. If it is not done, the efficiency of our industrial and commercial civilization can be sustained only by means of a system of controls which will be not free enterprise but national socialism and dictatorship.

When a hundred or a thousand or a hundred thousand

men work together under the management of a single plant or corporation, no medium ever devised can awaken in all of them a real understanding of the things they need to know if they are to co-operate efficiently. As long as they are viewed and dealt with as units of a hundred or a thousand or a hundred thousand, the best result which can be obtained is co-ordination of their efforts through direction and discipline, which is fundamentally different from spontaneous co-operation under accepted leadership.

Through six generations of our national history, we have adhered to an ideal of individual liberty. We have expressed the ideal in many phrases, all of which mean the same thing in terms of basic belief. They mean that we look upon the individual human being as the only important and lasting element in society. They mean that we accept and approve of government, industrial organization, corporations, unions, and all other groupings and mechanisms only as agencies to promote the interest of the individual person. All our expressions of the ideal are confessions of faith in achievement through individual growth, ability and co-operation, not through regimentation and direction from supergovernment or superman.

This ideal demands individuals who understand, and whose energies are released from within because they understand. Even the structure of political democracy cannot stand firmly on the foundation of an electorate whose individual members do not understand, do not think and feel as understanding human beings. The ink is not yet dry on the chapters of history which record the surrender of the rights of sacred personality by hundreds of millions of people who have submitted to dictation and regimentation. They have submitted because they had come to think of themselves no longer as individuals but as fractions of a class.

Industry has conditioned the mind of the average citizen toward this attitude, and has actually prepared him to vote away some of the most basic protections of his individual liberty. When we see a thousand clerks and salesgirls swarming out of a department store at quitting time, we see the workings of a school in which we have taught them to think of themselves as members of a mass, numbers on a payroll. When we see five thousand men going past the time clocks into a mammoth factory at the hour for changing shifts, going in so that five thousand others may come out, we have an object lesson in mass consciousness. When we go inside and see four hundred of them, standing in ranks before identical machines, making identical motions at identical intervals, we have an advanced lesson in regimentation. And when employers undertake to supply information to the thousand or five thousand or four hundred, in any uniform way, those employers have themselves accepted the religion of regimentation. They have confessed the faith that a mass of men can be led to mass thinking as they have been led to mass production.

Practically all the media for sharing information with employees which we have discussed in previous chapters are used to convey the same information, in the same way, at the same time, to employees as a mass. We have offered the opinion that this does not create understanding, that it does not effectively convey information, but that it can create interest in the minds of individual employees. We have maintained that interest so created will manifest itself in questions, and that the channel for discussing those questions should be identical with the channel through which work-knowledge passes, the so-called line of supervision.

The final outlet of this channel can be the "understanding unit" in modern industry, a lead man associated with a small number of fellow workers. Such a grouping already exists in every well-organized plant in business or industry. It exists because practical experience and scientific research have both proved the necessity of such a unit, for the adequate organization of men to work together.

This working unit or working group may be an electrical crew of five to eight on "line maintenance." It is the twelve girls on the notion counter in the store. It is the six-man crew on the same shift in the boiler house and turbine room. It is the eleven men on the shipping or carloading crew, or the "gang" of longshoremen. It is the district sales force for the vacuum-cleaner company, and the crew of seven men on the same shift in the oil refinery distillation unit or the saw-mill "side."

We find the "understanding unit" repeated in every successful organization for co-operative action of people outside industry. It is the group in the local church under the leadership of the deacon or deaconess. It is the seminar group in the graduate school of the university. It is the "cell" or "fraction" of the Communist party, the effective working unit even for the propagation of the doctrine of the class struggle! It is the football team or the baseball team.

In the largest of our mass-production industries it has been lost for the time being. It is returning. In one of the largest companies of this kind, five years ago, the working organization or line of supervision ended with one foreman over three hundred men. As the fruits of misunderstanding began to ripen, the "line" was extended to provide one foreman for each fifty workers. That company with its hundred thousand workers will probably go on toward the unit of practical size for personal contact. There is hope for an understanding democracy in the fact that other companies are seeing the necessity of thus fitting their "line" organization to match the possibilities of the human instinct of association.

Students of the theory of organization will smile at this crude reflection of the doctrine of the "span of control." The practical application of the doctrine is generally accepted among those who live in the actual levels of performance. They know instinctively that the number of men who can be effectively led by one supervisor is limited. The number is larger when the tasks to be accomplished are routine or repetitive, smaller where individual thinking is required. Even in the army, the ultimate tactical unit is the squad.

When the task to be accomplished is understanding, the highest degree of individual thinking is required. The unit, therefore, must be relatively small. Thinking is not done in groups of any size. It can be done and can be stimulated and guided, in the minds of individuals in a small group. It cannot be generated as a rule in the individual minds, massed in a large group. The audience of five thousand listening to the political orator can be stimulated to action through their emotions but not through their minds.

The limit on the number which makes an "understanding unit" applies at all levels of the line of supervision. In an industrial organization whose working unit is eight men and a straw boss, we have the structure of an "understanding unit." If there are fifty such units and the fifty strawbosses all report directly to one superintendent or foreman, there is a hopeless break in the chain of understanding. It is just as necessary for the leaders of the basic units to be grouped into "understanding units" themselves as it is for the men who work under their leadership. No superman or master mind can create understanding in a group of fifty foremen. He cannot come much closer to it than can the old-school employer who deludes himself in the belief that because he knows his thousand employees each by name they understand him and his policies and problems.

A prominent official in the organized labor movement once told me how this effective unit had been part and parcel of his twenty years of union leadership. Whether in a local union, in a large employee unit, or in a federation, he had made it a practice to organize what he called "a chain of fives." He first selected five associates with whom he maintained close personal contact. Each of these in turn was required to select five others, who became his personal responsibility for purposes of information, instruction, and leadership in action. If necessary the chain was further multiplied, always in links of five.

A leading manufacturer of one of our great modern products was having labor trouble. He was talking with a friend of mine, a man as successful as the manufacturer but much wiser in some ways. The troubled manufacturer was expressing his sorrow and surprise at the lack of understanding shown by his antagonistic employees. The other man tried, carefully and sympathetically, to point out one of the causes:

"Malcolm, I remember you told me you had six men working with you on the first really successful model you built. If you will think back, those men were really working with you. You were working with them. They knew how you had to risk and pledge and sacrifice to get their wages for them. They knew most of the physical and technical and cost problems. They knew what was to become of that model if it worked, and that its success meant an order for twenty-five more, a year of steady work for them and twenty other men. Above all, they knew you.

"You have done a magnificent job since then. The order came for the twenty-five, then for thousands of others. Your six men are now six thousand. But they don't know they are working with you; they think they are working for you. They know nothing of your technical or financial problems, nothing of your sales outlook or your sources of material or the research problem of keeping ahead of your competitors. Above all, they don't know you, except as a name over the plant and in the newspapers.

"With all the great growth you have made in volume and in product development through research, you have neglected one thing. The close relationship between you and the first six men has become a great gulf between you and the six thousand. They can never know you personally, as did the first six who worked with you. And you have neglected, among all the splendid things you have done, to create or foster any chain of relationship between you and the six thousand as a substitute for the personal contact and understanding between you and the first six."

And the great manufacturer responded, in a flash of brilliant ignorance:

"I get the idea! I'll have a loud-speaker system installed tomorrow, so I can sit in my office and talk to all the boys in the plant at once!"

My friend claims that he restrained both his amusement and his irritation:

"No, Malcolm, they still would not know you. But they do know a hundred foremen and about four hundred lead men. Isn't it possible for the other thousands to get to know you, your plans and your problems, through these foremen and straw bosses? Especially the lead men; each of them is directly in contact with a dozen or fifteen workers."

"No," said the great industrialist, "I guess those fellows don't know me either."

That fact suggested the beginning of a sound program of building toward understanding, a real relationship between top management and the line supervisors, and the natural release of information and knowledge through the contacts which necessarily exist between the line supervisor and his small group of fellow workers.

But the building could not be done by trying to establish direct contacts, close enough and continuous enough, between the president and the five hundred line supervisors. What should have been built and maintained through twenty years could not now be quickly built.

But closest to the president was a group of plant executives who were already a scientifically correct unit by the theory of the "span of control." Nine functional executives were a group with whom the president could, and in fact did, maintain close and effective contact, on problems of design, production, cost, plant facilities, and marketing. With this same group he must now begin to exchange ideas on human relationships, and on the extension to others of their and his comprehensive view of the whole enterprise.

After the new attitude had become the common possession of this "understanding unit" in top management, to each member of the group fell the task of forging a next link in the chain. Each of them must establish the same unity of understanding in a natural working unit of line supervisors with whom he was directly in contact. This group might be five or six or ten or twelve general foremen who, in their line of supervision, were under the leadership of one of the nine top executives. Another group of "understanding units," nine of them, must be thus led in the job of thinking as they had already been led in the job of work supervision.

Another stage of slow but lasting progress must be the conversion of the next group of natural units into groups of understanding thinkers. Around each foreman were clustered, in the line of supervision, three or four or six direct work supervisors — shift foremen, lead men, straw bosses, shipping clerks. From each foreman to each of these work supervisors associated with him must reach the new bond of understanding.

Finally, and only as the culmination of all these steps, the structure of understanding will reach its climax in the ultimate working group. Living daily with each of these work supervisors is a group of ten to twenty men. They already look to this lead man for guidance in their work, assignment of tasks, instructions as to methods, and for criticism, discipline, or encouragement. To this relationship must now be added a relationship of frankness as regards the larger aspects of the company program and policy.

In this new relationship, every employee can eventually learn, from his own immediate supervisor, the story of this manufacturer and the first radio or motorcycle or washing machine he built, the story of the anxious efforts of that man and the six fellow workers to turn out a job which would bring the order for twenty-five more. From this supervisor, in natural and casual daily conversation, he can come to know that three of the original six are still with the company, and that one of them is Old Sour Puss, the night super.

But at the start the working bosses themselves did not know these facts. Not even the foremen, not even all nine of the top executives, knew them. At the beginning, the worker in the group of twelve or fifteen didn't care. To him the president was a name, identified with wealth and power and hardness. When the information has filtered through, from one "understanding unit" to another, perhaps a bulletin may announce an observance next Saturday of the twentieth anniversary of the business, or the retirement of Old Sour Puss, or the award of souvenirs to others of the original six on their completion of twenty years in the organization. If the "understanding unit" has come to life within the natural working unit, the lead man will be asked who worked here when the company started? What became of them? Was the president already a rich man then? Did he really invent the product or did he buy the patents? Did he ever work, himself?

If the "understanding unit" has been recognized and fostered, every legitimate medium for sharing information with employees will create new opportunities for the building of understanding. The "understanding unit" will be a builder of understanding without any of the conventional media, without a house organ or bulletin board or "president's letter" or employee meeting. And with suitable use of good media, the building of understanding, in the "understanding unit," through the line supervision, will be infinitely more rapid and extensive. If the "understanding unit" has not been recognized and cultivated, if line supervision has not been adopted and prepared as the master medium for sharing information, all the house organs and personal letters in the world, all the other implements for sharing information, will fail to create understanding.

The "understanding unit" must come back into industry. When it does, we shall have recaptured the soul of that old furniture shop. Without destroying the efficiency of modern big business, the pooling of capital, the productiveness of great industrial plants, we shall have restored the living, understanding relationship of the good old days. We shall have, among the thousands of workers of the great factory, hundreds of the "understanding units" into which our grandfathers put their strength and their interest, because they knew, and understood!